KT-398-807

50 RECIPES FOR

COLOURFUL
WINDOW BOXES

COLOURFUL WINDOW BOXES

RICHARD BIRD

WARD LOCK

A WARD LOCK BOOK

First published in the UK 1997 by Ward Lock
Wellington House, 125 Strand
London WC2R 0BB

A Cassell Imprint

Copyright © Ward Lock 1997

All rights reserved. No part of this publication may be reproduced in any material form (including photocopying or storing it in any medium by electronic means and whether or not transiently or incidentally to some other use of this publication) without the written permission of the copyright owner, except in accordance with the provisions of the Copyright, Designs and Patents Act 1988 or under the terms of a licence issued by the Copyright Licensing Agency, 90 Tottenham Court Road, London W1P 9HE. Applications for the copyright owner's written permission to reproduce any part of this publication should be addressed to the publisher.

Distributed in the United States
by Sterling Publishing Co., Inc.
387 Park Avenue South, New York, NY 10016–8810

Distributed in Canada
by Cavendish Books Inc., Unit 5, 801 West 1st Street
North Vancouver, B.C., Canada V7P 1PH

A British Library Cataloguing in Publication Data block for this book
may be obtained from the British Library

ISBN 0 7063 7492 4

Designed by Richard Carr
Printed and bound in Spain

Contents

Introduction

WHAT SHOULD THE well-dressed house be wearing this year? Here are 50 recipes to help you make up your mind. They range from the frivolous to the sophisticated – everything, in fact, to suit your house and your mood.

But why should you bother to create a window box? Simply because it is a way of changing the mood and character of your house, as well as a way of cheering up those who live in it and pass by it. Some houses have so much personality of their own that do not need anything extra, but the majority of houses will benefit immeasurably from the addition of a window box or two, in the same way that a room benefits from the introduction of pictures and ornaments.

A perfect window box with a colourful display of flower power that completely hides the container.

A cold, white-washed exterior can be warmed by the use of colourful plants. A plain house may be made to look more sophisticated by the controlled use colours and elegant shapes. These changes are not permanent. Unlike painting a house, you can quickly undo your work if you get bored with it or if you decide it does not suit you or your home. You can, of course, clothe the walls in creepers and climbing plants, but these can take years to become established, and they are, in any case, more on a par with painting your house. On the other hand, window boxes allow you to give in to your whims and to decorate the façade with all kinds of bright colours that you would never dare do in paint or with more permanent plantings.

Creating window boxes is more than just a way of 'deco-rating' your house; it can do a lot for you as well. It not only gives you the satisfaction of creating something that was not there before, but also gives you the pleasure of enjoying your handiwork over a long period of time, no matter whether it is raining, snowing, windy or sunny. There is nothing more enjoyable to someone sitting inside on a cold, grey day than to see, just beyond the glass, a forest of golden daffodils, making it appear that the sun is permanently shining. And think of the passers-by. There are few more pleasurable things than walking down a street where the houses have attractive window boxes.

'Attractive' does not mean garish, and you do not have to fill a window box with bright colours to feel that you have been 'successful'. It can also mean simple plantings, with soft colours that are sympathetic to the house. 'Attractive' can, in fact, mean anything you like: the choice is yours, and you are in control.

A window box for late autumn made up of greens, reds and purples, enlivened by the mask with carex hair.

Window box gardens are not expensive to create and maintain. The costliest item is the box itself, but reasonably inexpensive plastic versions are available, and once you have got them they will last for many years. If you are a handyman or know someone who is, boxes can be run up quite cheaply from scraps of wood. Plants can be expensive, but compare their cost with that of cut flowers and bear in mind that they last a great deal longer. You can, of course, raise your own plants. Packets of seed of all kinds are relatively cheap and widely available, and you can always swap some of the packet, or the resulting seedlings, with a friend or a neighbour to help spread the costs.

Not all window box gardeners have the time or the skill to create their own schemes. This book provides a starting point. In it are 50 different recipes for a successful display. If you are a newcomer to window box gardening, you can follow these suggestions and find that you will have created something beautiful for yourself. When you have followed a few of the recipes here, you will soon begin to feel your own

way and want to create your own designs. At first, you may make one or two simple modifications to one of the recipes in this book, but gradually you will acquire the confidence to step out on your own and choose the plants and the way that you use them.

Each recipe contains enough information to create a window box similar to the one illustrated. There are details of the ingredients required and the way to plant up the box. These recipes are far from sacrosanct, however, and you should feel free to make any modifications you want. It may be that your window box is a different shape or size from the one shown, so you will want to use more or fewer plants in it. Your local garden centre or nursery may have in stock plants that are not in the recipe but that you would like to use. Perhaps you would like a similar display but would prefer different colours. By all means experiment as much as you wish.

Spring Charm

*T*HIS CHARMING BOX *is full of all the ingredients of a spring garden – primroses, tulips, daffodils and scillas. The daffodils and tulips are sensibly kept to a smaller scale so that they do not dwarf the lower growing primroses. The colours range from bright reds to soft pinks, from blues to white and with all shades of yellow. In a border such a riot of colour would look too jumbled, but here they blend beautifully to remind us that summer is only just around the corner.*

INGREDIENTS

12 early pink tulips (*Tulipa* 'Peach Blossom') **(A)**
20 daffodil bulbs (*Narcissus* 'Tête-à-Tête') **(B)**
6 blue scillas (*Scilla sibirica* 'Spring Beauty') **(C)**
12 mixed-coloured primroses (*Primula* 'Show Mixture') **(D)**

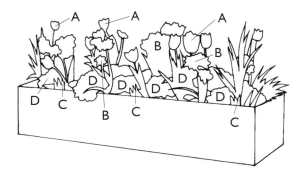

CONTAINER

Wooden window box with an inner plastic box
60cm (24in) long; 20cm (8in) wide; 20cm (8in) deep

MATERIALS

Pieces of broken pots or tiles
2.5cm (1in) layer of gravel or small stones
General potting compost to fill container

POSITION

A sunny position is needed, but preferably one that does not get too hot.

PLANTING

1. The bulbs can be planted in autumn, but mark spaces for the primroses. These can be planted at the same time if the plants are ready or put into the box as they come into flower, just before positioning it on the window-sill.

2. The drainage holes in the window box or its liner should be partially covered with a piece of broken pot.

3. To help with the drainage cover the bottom 2.5cm (1in) with a layer of gravel or small stones.

4. Half fill the rest of the box with compost.

5. Position the tulips and daffodils in random groups around the window box, leaving spaces for the primulas. Place the scillas in three groups along the front of the box. Fill the rest of the box with compost, starting at one end and planting the primroses as you go so that you do not plant them on top of the bulbs.

6. Firm down the compost so that the surface is 2.5cm (1in) below the top of the box.

7. Water.

MAINTENANCE

Keep the compost moist without making it soaking wet. Feed once a week.

Spring Joy

*T*HE FOCAL POINT *of this wonderful spring display is undoubtedly the splendid cineraria in the centre. It is complemented by the red primrose hybrids tucked in tightly next to it and the two taller German primroses just behind these. The sides of this old terracotta window box have been left exposed so that its colour and texture can be appreciated. It is usually best to cover the sides of a window box because they would otherwise become too dominant in such a small display.*

INGREDIENTS

1 deep pink cineraria (*Perilla × hybrida*) **(A)**
2 red primrose hybrids (*Primula* 'Silver Lining') **(B)**
2 German primroses (*Primula obconica*) **(C)**
2 arrow-leaved ivies (*Hedera helix* 'Sagittifolia') **(D)**
3 windflowers (*Anemone blanda* 'White Splendour') **(E)**

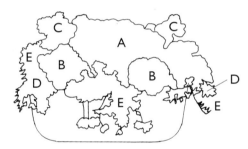

CONTAINER

Terracotta window box with rounded ends
45cm (18in) long; 15cm (6in) wide; 17.5cm (7in) deep

MATERIALS

Pieces of old pottery or broken roof tiles
2.5cm (1in) layer of gravel or small stones
General potting compost to fill container

POSITION

Although this container would tolerate some shade, it will look best in a sunny position as long as it is not too hot.

PLANTING

1. It would be difficult to plant this up in advance and get everything to come into flower at the right time. It is best to plant it when everything is already in bloom or is just on the point of flowering.

2. Put pieces of old crock over the drainage holes to stop the gravel and compost falling through.

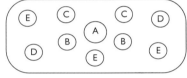

3. Cover the crocks and bottom of the window box with a layer of gravel or small stones to help keep the container free from excess water.

4. Fill the box with a general compost.

5. Start by planting the cineraria in the centre of the box. Then, being careful not to damage the cineraria, tuck the red primroses under its skirts, with the taller German primroses behind. Find space for an ivy at each end, and finally add the anemones, which will have to be tucked in tight under the other plants.

6. If there is room, firm down the compost; if not, tap the box on a table or the ground a few times to settle it.

7. Water.

MAINTENANCE

Water regularly. Daily watering will be necessary when the weather is sunny and warm. Feed twice a week. Remove any dead flowers as they appear.

Colourful Spring

THESE BOXES ARE burgeoning with spring colours. So often at this time of year, flower colour is restricted to shades of yellow, but here reds, pinks, mauves and white blend with a variety of foliage colours to give a most delightful display, especially when seen against the whiteness of the wall behind. In addition to the variety of colours, there is an abundance of different shapes and textures, all contained within a small space. Two boxes have been used instead of one, but they merge together to create a single, unified display.

INGREDIENTS

3 red florist's cyclamen (*Cyclamen*) **(A)**
4 pink florist's cyclamen (*Cyclamen*) **(B)**
2 purple florist's cyclamen (*Cyclamen*) **(C)**
4 variegated hebes (*Hebe × franciscana* 'Variegata') **(D)**
2 white German primroses (*Primula obconica*) **(E)**
2 mauve German primroses (*Primula obconica*) **(F)**
2 dwarf conifers (*Thuja*) **(G)**
2 white heathers (*Calluna vulgaris* 'Spring Cream') **(H)**
1 variegated euonymus (*Euonymus japonicus* 'Président Gauthier') **(I)**
1 white marguerite (*Argyranthemum frutescens*) **(J)**
3 trailing ivies (*Hedera helix* 'Eva') **(K)**

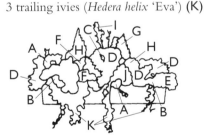

CONTAINERS

2 terracotta containers
Each container 45cm (18in) long; 15cm (6in) wide; 15cm (6in) deep

MATERIALS

Pieces of old pottery or tile
2.5cm (1in) layer of gravel
Lime-free (ericaceous) compost to fill containers

POSITION

Either semi-shade or a sunny position will be suitable.

PLANTING

1. Plant up the window boxes in winter or spring as the plants are coming into flower.

2. Cover the drainage holes with broken pottery or tiles to prevent the gravel from falling through. To further improve drainage, cover the bottom of each container with 2.5cm (1in) layers of gravel.

3. Fill the containers with lime-free compost.

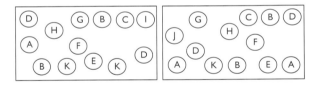

4. Start by planting the plants in the back row of each box. The cyclamens can be planted in winter if the boxes are kept frost free; otherwise insert them in spring. Plant the cyclamen to the same depth as they are in the pots – that is, with the corm just below the surface. Alternatively, plunge the entire pot into the compost. Work forwards, positioning each plant as indicated on the plan.

5. Firm down the compost around the plants and level it so that the surface is just below the rim. Water.

MAINTENANCE

Water regularly. Protect cyclamen and marguerites from late frosts.

Simple Contrasts

*T*HIS IS A *good example of how a simple planting can create an extremely effective display. The colour contrast between the white hyacinths and the stripy tulips is excellent. The lax habit of the hyacinths echoes the leaves of the tulips and at the same time contrasts with the stiffness of the tulip stems, while the open nature of the hyacinth flowers contrasts with the strong shapes of the tulips. If the display has a drawback, it is that it is short-lived.*

INGREDIENTS

12 striped, strongly coloured tulips (*Tulipa* 'Sundance') **(A)**
14 white multiflorus hyacinths (*Hyacinthus* 'White Pearl') **(B)**

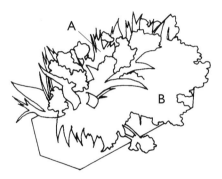

CONTAINER

Wooden or plastic window box, preferably black
or dark green
60cm (24in) long; 20cm (8in) wide; 20cm (8in) deep

MATERIALS

Pieces of old crocks or tiles
2.5cm (1in) layer of gravel
General potting compost to fill container

POSITION

Any position will do, although it will look best in sun. A
white wall provides an ideal background.

PLANTING

1. Plant the container in autumn before the bulbs come into growth.

2. Cover the drainage holes with a piece of broken pottery so that the compost cannot fall out yet excess water can drain away.

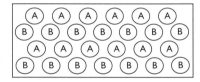

3. Improve the drainage by filling the bottom 2.5cm (1in) with gravel or small stones.

4. Half fill the container with compost.

5. Lay out the bulbs. Fill the box with compost so that the bulbs are covered by compost at least 5cm (2in) deep.

6. Gently press down the compost and level it off so that the surface is about 2.5cm (1in) below the top of the box.

7. Water and put to one side.

8. Position the window box just as the bulbs come into flower.

MAINTENANCE

No maintenance is required as long as the box is in a position where it can get rain. Water in prolonged dry periods. Plant out the bulbs in the garden when the display is over. This display can be planted in a plastic container that can be slipped inside a more decorative window box when the bulbs come into flower.

Pretty Primulas

*P*RIMROSES AND POLYANTHUS *are great symbols of spring. Everyone welcomes them not only for their own sake, but because they herald the end of winter and better things to come. In this unusual display they have been combined with silver cinerarias, plants more often associated with summer. The display is given substance by a golden poor-man's box, and the dainty leaved ivies provide the perfect finishing touch. This is not a long-lived display, but it will give plenty of pleasure while it lasts.*

INGREDIENTS

1 golden poor-man's box (*Lonicera nitida* 'Baggesen's Gold') **(A)**
7 mixed colour primrose and polyanthus hybrids (*Primula*) **(B)**
2 silver cinerarias (*Senecio cineraria* 'Silver Dust') **(C)**
2 trailing ivies (*Hedera helix* 'Sagittifolia') **(D)**

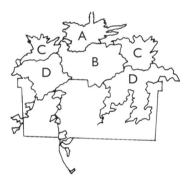

CONTAINER

Terracotta window box
45cm (18in) long; 15cm (6in) wide; 20cm (8in) deep

MATERIALS

Pieces of broken pottery or old bits of tile
2.5cm (1in) layer of gravel
General potting compost to fill container

POSITION

A sunny window-sill will be ideal.

PLANTING

1. It is best to prepare this box as the plants come into bloom so that you can be sure that they will all flower at the same time. The cinerarias might suffer in cold weather, so do not plant them out too early.

2. Cover the drainage holes with pieces of broken pot so that compost and gravel do not stop fall through.

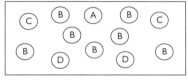

3. The bottom of the window box should be covered with a 2.5cm (1in) layer of gravel to improve drainage.

4. Fill the container with a general potting compost.

5. Begin by planting the poor-man's box at the centre back of the box. Position five of the primulas in a semicircle around it, arranging the colours to make a pattern if you wish. The cinerarias can be planted next, with the remaining primulas in front of them. Finish off by planting the ivies in the front but towards the ends of the container so that they can be encouraged to cascade over the three visible sides of the box.

6. Firm down the compost around the plants and level the surface so that it is 2.5cm (1in) below the rim of the box.

7. Water.

MAINTENANCE

Water when the soil begins to dry out. Discard after the primulas begin to fade.

Tête-à-Tête

*E*VERYONE LOOKS EAGERLY *for the first daffodils as a sign that the dark, gloomy days of winter are beginning to give way to the brighter days of spring and their promise that summer is not far behind. Here the daffodils are treated with great simplicity – they are mixed with a few double snowdrops and a foreground of ivy. The daffodils are relatively short so they not only go well with the lower growing snowdrops but are better able than their taller cousins to withstand wind, in what could be an exposed position.*

INGREDIENTS

36 daffodil bulbs (*Narcissus* 'Tête-à-Tête') **(A)**
18 double snowdrops (*Galanthus nivalis* 'Flore Pleno') **(B)**
3 variegated ivies (*Hedera helix* 'Glacier') **(C)**

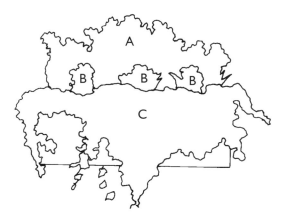

CONTAINER

Wooden window box, painted black
60cm (24in) long; 15cm (6in) wide; 20cm (8in) deep

MATERIALS

Pieces of broken pottery or bits of old roof tiles
2.5cm (1in) layer of gravel
General potting compost to fill container

POSITION

A sunny site will be perfect.

PLANTING

1. It is best to plant up this container once the bulbs are in flower, which will be in late winter.

2. Cover the drainage holes with pieces of old pottery so that the water can still escape but the compost and gravel are prevented from falling through and blocking the holes.

3. Fill the bottom 2.5cm (1in) of the window box with a layer of gravel to help improve drainage.

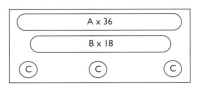

4. Fill the box with a general potting compost.

5. If the bulbs are already in flower when you plant them you can arrange the daffodils as in the picture, with the tallest in the centre, grading down in size at each end. The daffodils should be grown on in pots (planted in early autumn) and planted out either as a clump or even left in their pots, which can be plunged into the compost. The snowdrops can similarly be grown in pots and planted out as clumps. These are planted in front of the daffodils with the ivies being set out along the front of the box.

6. Firm down the compost if the bulbs have been taken out of their pots.

7. Water.

MAINTENANCE

There is little maintenance except for occasional watering.

Cyclamen Colour

*C*YCLAMEN ARE WONDERFUL *plants for a winter window box, particularly in towns, where winter temperatures do not fall too low. Even in areas subject to cold snaps, if the cyclamen are left in their pots they can be moved inside until the cold weather has passed. Here the glowing colours of the cyclamen are set off against a background of the dense foliage of ivies, hebes and heathers. The clematis climb over the plants and hang from the box during summer, further illuminating the foliage plants.*

INGREDIENTS

5 pink florist's cyclamen (*Cyclamen*) **(A)**
2 red florist's cyclamen (*Cyclamen*) **(B)**
1 variegated ivy (*Hedera helix* 'Eva') **(C)**
1 variegated euonymus (*Euonymus japonicus* 'Aureus') **(D)**
2 variegated hebes (*Hebe × franciscana* 'Variegata') **(E)**
2 winter-flowering heathers (*Erica carnea* 'Vivellii') **(F)**
2 summer-flowering heathers (*Erica cinerea* 'C.D. Eason') **(G)**
2 large-flowered clematis (*Clematis* 'Lasurstern') **(H)**

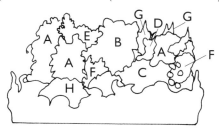

CONTAINER

Wooden window box
90cm (3ft) long; 25cm (10in) wide; 15cm (6in) deep

MATERIALS

Pieces of broken tile or pot
2.5cm (1in) layer of gravel
Lime-free (ericaceous) compost to fill container

POSITION

This window box is suitable for a shady wall, but will also do well in the sun.

PLANTING

1. Plant this box in autumn. Leave gaps for the cyclamen and insert them, still in their pots when they are in flower.

2. Cover the drainage holes of the window box with pieces of broken pottery or irregular stones so that excess water can pass through without washing away the compost.

3. Add a 2.5cm (1in) layer of gravel to help with drainage.

4. Fill the box with lime-free compost.

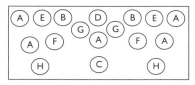

5. Start either by planting the cyclamen or by marking where they are to go if you want to plant them when they are in flower. Next plant the variegated hebes and the euonymus at the back of the box as shown on the plan. Next to the euonymus plant the summer-flowering heathers. In the front corners plant the clematis, but do not include the canes because they are to sprawl rather than climb. Finally, plant the two winter-flowering heathers and the variegated ivy.

6. Firm in the soil around the plants and level the compost to just below the edge of the box.

7. Water.

MAINTENANCE

Watering is more necessary in summer than spring unless the weather is dry. Train the clematis so that they flow round and over the other plants.

Summer Brightness

T̲ʜɪꜱ ʙᴏx, ꜱᴇᴇɴ here before it is moved into position, will brighten even the dullest of days. The centre-piece is a bright red begonia, and the geraniums and other plants form a pyramid of colour around it, while the slender, floating stems of the lobelias bring a light, airy feel to the whole arrangement. The colour of the terracotta container fits in well with the colour scheme and looks better than a wooden one would.

INGREDIENTS

1 bright red begonia (*Begonia* 'Flame') **(A)**
2 pink geraniums (*Pelargonium* 'Ascot') **(B)**
2 young fuchsias (*Fuchsia* 'Dark Eyes') **(C)**
1 pink godetia (*Clarkia* 'Pink Joy') **(D)**
1 white godetia (*Clarkia* 'Snowflake') **(E)**
4 mixed lobelias (*Lobelia*) **(F)**

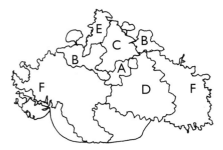

CONTAINER

Decorated terracotta container
45cm (18in) long; 17.5cm (7in) wide; 17.5cm (7in) deep

MATERIALS

Pieces of old pottery or broken pieces of tile
2.5cm (1in) layer of gravel
Lime-free (ericaceous) compost to fill container

POSITION

This display will be best suited to a warm, sunny position.

PLANTING

1. Plant up the container in early summer, once frosts are no longer a threat. It can be planted earlier and kept under glass so that it is in full flower when moved out.

2. Use pieces of old pottery to cover the drainage holes so that the gravel does not fall out but so that excess water can easily drain away.

3. Cover the bottom of the window box with a 2.5cm (1in) layer of gravel to help improve the drainage.

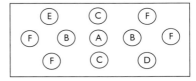

4. Use a lime-free compost to fill the container; begonias prefer lime-free conditions.

5. Start in the centre by planting the begonia. On either side of this set the two pink geraniums. In front of one geranium and behind the other, plant the two godetias so that they are diagonally opposite one another. One of the small fuchsias is planted in front of, and the other behind, the begonia. The remaining space is filled with the lobelias.

6. Lightly press down the compost around the plants and level the surface so that it is just below the rim of the window box.

7. Water.

MAINTENANCE

Water regularly – at least once a day in hot weather – and feed once a week. Any dead flowers should be taken off as they appear.

One in the Eye

THIS IS A LARGE display made up of two boxes, placed end to end to make one long display. Only one box is shown here. The other box is a mirror image of the first so that they appear as a symmetrical, unified whole. Although the colour is provided by mixture of garden flowers, the white daisies that form the centrepiece are a good form of the wild ox-eye daisy or marguerite. The white flowers cool the busy scene, which seems to contain examples of most of the different types of plants usually associated with window boxes.

INGREDIENTS

(Double the quantity for both boxes)
4 white ox-eye daisies (*Leucanthemum vulgare*) **(A)**
3 mixed-coloured busy lizzies (*Impatiens*) **(B)**
1 purple ivy-leaved geranium (*Pelargonium* 'Amethyst') **(C)**
1 pink fuchsia (*Fuchsia* 'Tennessee Waltz') **(D)**
1 purple petunia (*Petunia*) **(E)**
1 pink petunia (*Petunia*) **(F)**
3 blue lobelias (*Lobelia* 'Blue Wave') **(G)**
2 variegated helichrysums (*Helichrysum petiolare* 'Variegatum') **(H)**

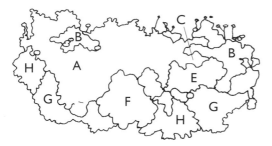

CONTAINERS

2 wooden window boxes, painted cream
Each box 60cm (24in) long; 20cm (8in) wide; 17.5cm (7in) deep

MATERIALS

Pieces of broken pottery or old roof tiles
2.5cm (1in) layer of gravel
General potting compost to fill containers

POSITION

A sunny position is required for this display.

PLANTING

1. Plant up the boxes in late spring or early summer.

2. To prevent the drainage material from falling through the holes, cover them with pieces of broken pottery or tile.

3. Fill the bottom 2.5cm (1in) with gravel or small stones to help with drainage.

4. Loosely fill the window boxes with a general potting compost.

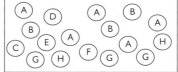

5. Start by positioning the daisies as shown on the plan (remember to reverse the positions for the second box). Next plant the busy lizzies. The geraniums come next, planted at one end of each box. The fuchsias go towards the centres of each arrangement. The boxes are already becoming full, so be careful when you put in the petunias, because it is easy to damage their stems. The helichrysums can then be positioned, with the lobelias tucked into the gaps.

6. Level the compost just below the rim of the box.

7. Water.

MAINTENANCE

Water once a day and feed twice a week. Replace the daisies with white argyranthemums when they fade.

Petunia Surprise

*T*HIS CONFECTION OF *colours looks almost good enough to eat! At first glance it seems to be a compli-cated planting scheme, but it is, in fact, made up of just three types of plant – petunias, lobelias and geraniums. Two kinds of petunias are used. Trailing varieties have been placed near the front, while conventional bedding petunias are included at the back. Although the petunias and the geraniums provide the colour, it is the two blocks of white and pink lobelias that catch the eye and unify the whole display.*

INGREDIENTS

2 pink lobelias (*Lobelia* 'Pink Fountain') (A)
3 trailing petunias (*Petunia* 'Super Cascade') (B)
5 bedding petunias (*Petunia* 'Falcon Mixed') (C)
1 pink ivy-leaved geranium (*Pelargonium* 'Dresdner Rosalit') (D)
1 scarlet zonal geranium (*Pelargonium* ' Paul Crampel') (E)
1 white zonal geranium (*Pelargonium* 'Glacis') (F)
1 salmon-pink zonal geranium (*Pelargonium* 'King of Denmark') (G)
1 continental ivy-leaved geranium (*Pelargonium* 'Lilac Mini Cascade') (H)

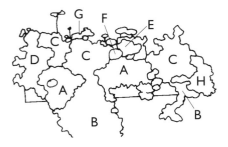

CONTAINER

2 wooden containers, joined together to make a single box
Overall size 120cm (48in) long; 15cm (6in) wide; 20cm (8in) deep

MATERIALS

Pieces of old broken pottery or irregularly shaped stones
2.5cm (1in) layer of gravel or grit
General potting compost to fill containers

POSITION

A sunny position, away from the wind is best.

PLANTING

1. Do not plant the window boxes until early summer, when the threat of frost has passed, unless you are able to do it under glass and move it out later.

2. The drainage holes should be partially covered with pieces of pot so that the compost does not fall out.

3. Cover the crocks and the bottom of the boxes with gravel to improve the drainage.

4. Fill the boxes with a general potting compost.

5. The order and position of planting is not critical, but it is a good idea to keep the pale colours to one side and the richer ones to the other. First plant the petunias, with the bedding varieties at the back and the trailing ones at the front. Petunias are brittle, so be careful. Next plant the geraniums and finally the lobelias.

6. Firm down the compost and level it just below the rim of the box.

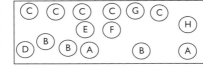

7. Water.

MAINTENANCE

Water at least once a day and feed twice a week. Keep the display tidy.

Golden Surprise

*T*HIS EYE-CATCHING DISPLAY *would brighten up even the dreariest of summer's days. It does, however, owe something to the florist's art, because not all these flowers are naturally in flower at the same time in the garden. The chrysanthemums, for example, would normally flower well after the brooms, but if plants are purchased in flower as pot plants from a florist or garden centre, this stunning show can easily be created.*

INGREDIENTS

1 cream and yellow broom (*Cytisus scoparius* 'Cornish Cream') **(A)**
2 variegated abutilons (*Abutilon* 'Savitzii') **(B)**
1 golden-yellow chrysanthemum (*Dendranthema*) **(C)**
2 pale yellow chrysanthemums (*Dendranthema*) **(D)**
3 golden brooms (*Cytisus* × *praecox* 'Allgold') **(E)**
4 variegated ivies (*Hedera helix* 'Eva') **(F)**

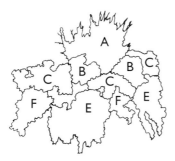

CONTAINER

Wooden window box, painted white
90cm (36in) long; 20cm (8in) wide; 20cm (8in) deep

MATERIALS

Pieces of broken pottery or old bits of tile
2.5cm (1in) layer of gravel
General potting compost to fill container

POSITION

A sunny aspect will be best for this display.

PLANTING

1. This box will have to be planted in late spring or early summer, when the plants are in flower.

2. So that the compost and gravel does not trickle through the drainage holes, cover them with crocks. There should be sufficient gaps for any excess water to trickle away.

3. Cover the bottom of the box with a 2.5cm (1in) layer of gravel or small stones to help improve the drainage.

4. Fill the container with a general potting compost.

5. This is a full box, so plant it tightly. Start with the 'Cornish Cream' broom,

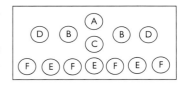

at the centre back of the box. At each side and slightly in front plant the abutilons. Next to come are the two pale yellow chrysanthemums. Tuck the golden-yellow chrysanthemum tight against the broom. Finally, plant the front row with ivies and the 'Allgold' broom.

6. If you cannot get among the plants to firm down the compost, tap it smartly on a table or the ground a few times to settle it down.

7. Arrange the flowing stems over the edge of the box.

8. Water.

MAINTENANCE

This box will need plenty of moisture, so water at least once a day, more in hot weather. Feed twice a week.

Gold and Blue

*T*HE COLOURING OF *this window box is more subtle than most, although it is still bright enough to attract attention. It is often a good idea to have a change from strong colours and choose something a little more restful. The yellow of the pansies and the soft blue of the petunias combine well together, and the marguerites form a good background without being overpowering. The trailing ivies and helichrysums finish off the display by spilling down over the front of the window box, blurring its hard lines.*

INGREDIENTS

3 white marguerites (*Argyranthemum frutescens*) **(A)**
4 yellow pansies (*Viola* 'Universal Yellow') **(B)**
3 blue petunias (*Petunia* 'Blue Skies') **(C)**
3 golden helichrysums (*Helichrysum petiolare* 'Limelight') **(D)**
2 variegated ivies (*Hedera helix* 'Glacier') **(E)**

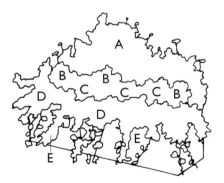

CONTAINER

Wooden window box, painted white
90cm (36in) long; 20cm (8in) wide; 20cm (8in) deep

MATERIALS

Pieces of broken pottery or pieces of old tile
2.5cm (1in) layer of gravel
General potting compost to fill container

POSITION

A sunny, protected site will be best for this display.

PLANTING

1. Start to prepare this window box in late spring or early summer, after the threat of frost has passed.

2. Use pieces of broken pottery to cover the drainage holes so that excess water can drain away while gravel and compost are not washed away.

3. Cover the bottom of the window box with a 2.5cm (1in) layer of gravel or small stones to help provide adequate drainage.

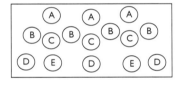

4. Fill the container with a general potting compost.

5. The white marguerites should be planted first. Position them against the back of the box, leaving room for the other plants. Next plant a row of alternating pansies and petunias, starting with the pansies. Place the petunias slightly in front. Finally, plant a row of alternating helichrysums and ivies, starting with a helichrysum, positioning them along the front so that they trail over the edge.

6. The compost should now be firmed gently down between the plants and the surface levelled off so that it is about 2.5cm (1in) below the rim of the box.

7. Water.

MAINTENANCE

Water once a day, more frequently during hot dry weather in midsummer. Feed twice a week. Remove any dead flowers.

Petunia Special

*P*ETUNIAS ARE THE *perfect plants for window boxes. They have an attractive colour range, usually with a velvety texture that gives the colours a rich quality, and young plants bear flowers and continue to do so right through summer and well into autumn, often until the first frost. Window boxes are particularly good places to grow them because the overhanging walls often afford some protection from rain, which can spoil the flowers of some of the older varieties. Here the display has been restricted to two varieties that enhance each other, and the container has been chosen to complement the window-frame and stonework.*

INGREDIENTS

3 white and red petunias (*Petunia* 'Red Picotee') **(A)**
2 purple petunias (*Petunia* 'Dwarf Resisto Blue') **(B)**
5 blue lobelias (*Lobelia* 'Blue Wave') **(C)**

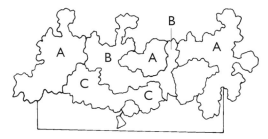

CONTAINER

Wooden window box, painted white
45cm (18in) long; 15cm (6in) wide; 15cm (6in) deep

MATERIALS

Pieces of old pottery or broken roof tiles
2.5cm (1in) layer of gravel
General potting compost to fill container

POSITION

A sunny window-sill would be the ideal place for this box.

PLANTING

1. Prepare the window box in late spring or early summer because late frosts can kill petunias.

2. The drainage holes should be partially covered with the broken pieces of pottery so that the compost and gravel cannot fall through, while excess water can still escape.

3. The bottom 2.5cm (1in) of the box should be filled with a layer of gravel to improve drainage.

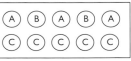

4. Fill the container with a general potting compost.

5. The planting of this box is straightforward, although care must be taken in handling the petunias, which have brittle stems that are easily broken. Plant them in a line across the box starting with a picotee variety and alternating with the purple. Fill the front of the box with lobelias.

6. Firm down the compost around the plants and level the surface so that it is about 2.5cm (1in) below the rim of the window box.

7. Water.

MAINTENANCE

Water regularly – at least once a day – and feed once a week. Petunias can look bedraggled if the dead flowers are left on, so remove them regularly.

A Regal Display

*W*HILE ZONAL AND *ivy-leaved geraniums are very popular window box plants, regal varieties are less commonly seen. This is a shame, because there are some very attractive plants in this category, such as the deep pink ones used here. They mix well with the trailing, pink-flowered, ivy-leaved geraniums and white and purple petunias. This display consists of three boxes, specially constructed to fit the three sides of a bay window.*

INGREDIENTS

1 white petunia (*Petunia* 'White Magic') **(A)**
2 purple petunias (*Petunia* 'Plum Purple') **(B)**
5 pink regal geraniums (*Pelargonium* 'Lavender Gram Slam') **(C)**
2 pink ivy-leaved geraniums (*Pelargonium* 'Amethyst') **(D)**
4 blue lobelias (*Lobelia* 'Blue Wave') **(E)**
2 variegated ivies (*Hedera helix* 'Eva') **(F)**

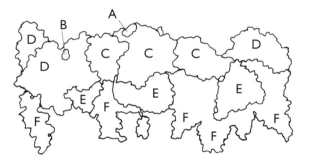

CONTAINER

Wooden container, painted white
120cm (4ft) long; 20cm (8in) wide; 20cm (8in) deep

MATERIALS

Pieces of broken pottery or pieces of old tile
2.5cm (1in) layer of gravel
General potting compost to fill container

POSITION

The geraniums will enjoy a sunny site.

PLANTING

1. Start to prepare this window box after the threat of frost has passed – late spring or early summer will be ideal.

2. Use the pieces of broken pottery to cover the drainage holes so that excess water can pass out but gravel and compost are not washed away.

3. Cover the bottom of the window box with a 2.5cm (1in) layer of gravel or small stones to help provide adequate drainage.

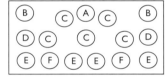

4. Fill the container with a general potting compost.

5. Plant the white petunia in the centre at the back so that it will gently spread out across the other plants. Next plant the two purple petunias in the back corners where they will have the same effect. The five regal geraniums can now be planted in the main part of the box. At each end plant the ivy-leaved geraniums. Finally fill in the front of the box with the lobelias and ivies, planting them so that they trail over the edge.

6. Firm down the compost between the plants and level the surface so that it is just below the top of the box.

7. Water.

MAINTENANCE

Water at least once a day and feed weekly. Remove any dead blooms as they appear.

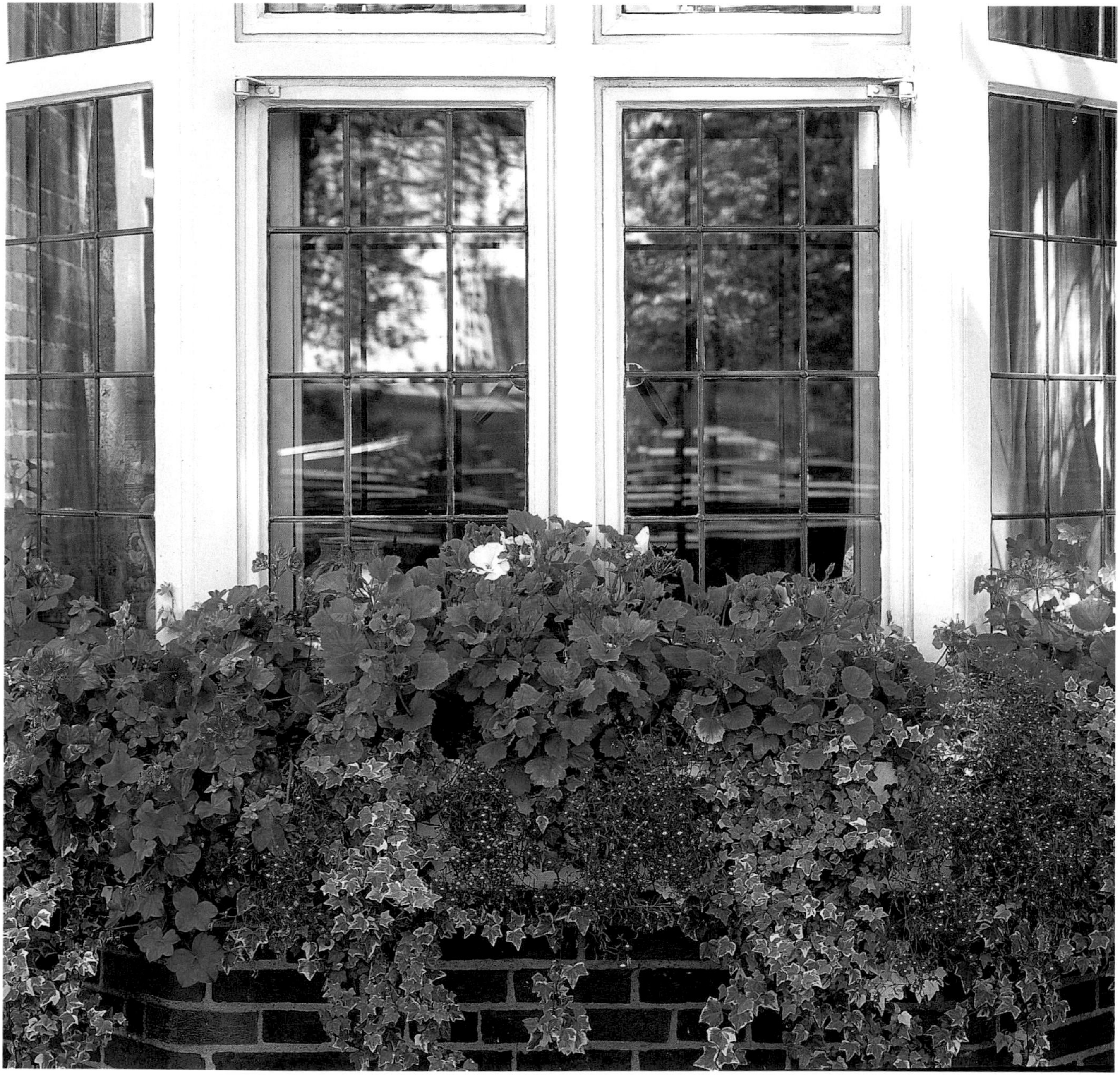

Solidarity

*T*HE MASS OF *attractive foliage gives this window box a lush, solid appearance. There is no space between the plants and they all become melded together in a beautiful whole. This is a display that will last and last, right through summer and well into autumn. In warmer areas and towns it might continue even longer. At the moment the dainty angel geraniums hold centre stage, but gradually the trailing geraniums will open up in a cascade of purple. The flanking scarlet geraniums frame the picture.*

INGREDIENTS

2 scarlet geraniums (*Pelargonium* 'Gustav Emich') **(A)**
5 angel geraniums (*Pelargonium* 'Manx Maid') **(B)**
3 ivy-leaved geraniums (*Pelargonium* 'Amethyst') **(C)**
4 variegated ground ivies (*Glechoma hederacea* 'Variegata') **(D)**
4 white verbenas (*Verbena* × *hybrida*) **(E)**

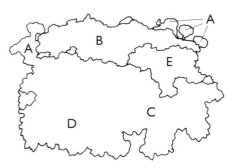

CONTAINER

Wooden window box
90cm (36in) long; 20cm (8in) wide; 20cm (8in) deep

MATERIALS

Pieces of broken pottery or irregularly shaped stones
2.5cm (1in) layer of gravel
General potting compost to fill container

POSITION

A bright sunny position is the best place for this display, although it will tolerate a little light shade.

PLANTING

1. Make up the box at the end of spring after the threat of frost has passed.

2. Cover the drainage holes with the broken pottery so that the gravel and compost cannot trickle out.

3. Fill the bottom of the box with a layer of gravel about 2.5cm (1in) deep to improve the drainage.

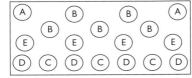

4. Fill the container to the rim with a general potting compost.

5. Start by planting the two scarlet geraniums in the corners of the box. Next plant the angel geraniums in two rows as shown in the plan. The verbenas come next, again in a row, just over half-way towards the front of the box. In front of these plant a row of alternating variegated ground ivy and trailing geraniums.

6. Gently firm the compost around the plants so that the final level is just below the rim of the pot.

7. Arrange the trailing foliage so that it hangs naturally down the front of the container.

8. Water.

MAINTENANCE

Water regularly and feed every 10 days. Remove any dead flowers or leaves as they appear.

Nasturtium Cascade

BY THE END of summer this window box will be producing a cascading display of flame red offset against the deep green of the foliage. The red is punctuated by small spots of bright magenta, not colours that usually sit happily together, but here they make a vibrant display when they are all in full bloom. Rows of geraniums and fuchsias in bright pinks and whites are the perfect foil for the waterfall of brighter colour. The window box is completely hidden by the mass of foliage and blooms, so it can be any colour or material.

INGREDIENTS

3 salmon-pink geraniums (*Pelargonium* 'Ascot') **(A)**
3 white geraniums (*Pelargonium* 'Queen of Whites') **(B)**
3 white fuchsias (*Fuchsia* 'Snow White') **(C)**
3 purple trailing petunias (*Petunia* 'Purple Surfinia') **(D)**
4 flame red nasturtiums (*Tropaeolum majus*) **(E)**

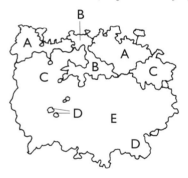

CONTAINER

Plain window box
90cm (36in) long; 20cm (8in) wide; 20cm (8in) deep

MATERIALS

Pieces of old pottery or broken pieces of tile
2.5cm (1in) layer of gravel
General potting compost to fill container
Water-retaining granules

POSITION

A bright sunny position is best for this display.

PLANTING

1. Plant up this container once the threat of frost has passed. Alternatively, it can be prepared in advance in a green-house and moved out once the weather is suitable.

2. Cover the drainage holes with broken pottery so that excess water can drain away but the compost is prevented from trickling out.

3. Cover the pottery and bottom of the box with a 2.5cm (1in) layer of gravel.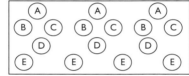

4. With this amount of foliage the plants will be constantly thirsty so help by mixing water-retaining granules with the compost and fill the container with the mixture.

5. At the back plant the three salmon-pink geraniums. Along the middle line of the box plant alternately the white geraniums and the fuchsias. The nasturtiums go along the front and tucked in behind these are the three trailing petunias.

6. Gently firm down the compost between the plants and level it so that the surface is just below the level of the box.

7. Arrange the foliage so that it trails naturally over the edge.

8. Water.

MAINTENANCE

Water regularly and feed once a week. Remove any dead flowers as they appear. This display can be badly mauled by wind, and it may be necessary to cut back the trailing stems .

Busy Lizzie

*T*HIS RICH DISPLAY *will remain full of foliage and flowers throughout summer and well into autumn. The most notable of the ingredients are the strong-growing busy lizzies. They can be all the same colour or, as here, mixed to give added interest. The cascade of blue lobelias creates a good contrast as it slips away beneath the busy lizzies. The young conifer in the middle creates a green centrepiece from which the other plants flow, completely hiding the sides of the box.*

INGREDIENTS

2 deep pink geraniums (*Pelargonium* 'Genie') **(A)**
1 young conifer (*Chamaecyparis*) **(B)**
4 mixed busy lizzies (*Impatiens*) **(C)**
6 blue lobelias (*Lobelia* 'Blue Wings') **(D)**

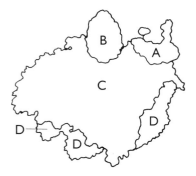

CONTAINER

Wooden window box
90cm (36in) long; 20cm (8in) wide; 20cm (8in) deep

MATERIALS

Pieces of old pottery or broken tiles
2.5cm (1in) layer of gravel
General potting compost
Water-retaining granules

POSITION

It is best to place this display out of sun when it is at its peak. Morning and afternoon sun or partial shade are ideal.

PLANTING

1. The best time to plant this container is in early summer.

2. Cover the drainage holes with pieces of broken pot so that excess water can drain away but the contents of the box cannot be washed out.

3. To help with drainage, cover the bottom of the container with a 2.5cm (1in) layer of gravel or small stones.

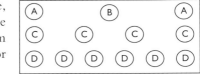

4. Because these plants require a lot of water, mix water-retaining granules with the compost.

5. Start at the back and plant the two pink geraniums in opposite corners, with the young conifer half-way between them. The four busy lizzies should be planted at equal intervals along the centre line of the box. If you are using mixed colours do not put two plants the same colour next to each other. Under these, along the front of the box, tuck in the six lobelias.

6. Firm the compost gently around the plants. Adding or removing compost as necessary, level the surface so that it is just below the edge of the box.

7. Water.

MAINTENANCE

Water once a day, especially during hot weather, and feed twice a week. Remove dead heads.

Summer Riches

T̲HIS IS AN *extremely effective display, mainly because of the rich colours of the flowers. The velvety purple of the petunias is always useful for giving an impression of richness and depth, and here it contrasts surprisingly well with the bright gold of the bidens, which seem to sparkle amid the depths of the dark foliage. The variegated foliage also helps to lighten the scene, while the lobelias, dark red geranium and blue felicia and Swan River daisy all help to make this a display of beauty and interest.*

INGREDIENTS

1 purple trailing petunia (*Petunia* 'Purple Surfinia') **(A)**
4 trailing bidens (*Bidens ferulifolia*) **(B)**
2 Swedish ivies (*Plectranthus coleoides* 'Marginatus') **(C)**
1 Swan River daisy (*Brachycome iberidifolia*) **(D)**
1 blue felicia (*Felicia amelloides*) **(E)**
1 scarlet geranium (*Pelargonium* 'Paul Crampel') **(F)**
1 pink geranium (*Pelargonium* 'Obergarten') **(G)**
2 trailing lobelias (*Lobelia* 'Blue Wings') **(H)**

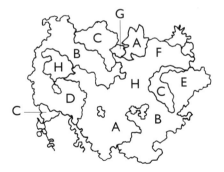

CONTAINER

Wooden container, painted a dark colour
90cm (36in) long; 15cm (6in) wide; 15cm (6in) deep

MATERIALS

Pieces of old pottery or broken tiles
2.5cm (1in) layer of gravel
General potting compost to fill container
Water-retaining granules

POSITION

A sunny position would be best for this colourful display.

PLANTING

1. The best time to plant this display is early summer because most of the plants are tender and will not tolerate frost.

2. The drainage holes should be covered with broken pieces of pottery so that excess water can escape, but the gravel and compost cannot fall out.

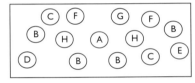

3. Aid the drainage by filling the bottom of the window box with a 2.5cm (1in) layer of gravel.

4. This will be a thirsty planting, so mix some water-retaining granules with the compost before filling the box.

5. Begin planting in the centre. Place the trailing petunia here. Be careful not to break its brittle stems. Next space the four bidens across the box. Plant the Swan River daisy and the felicia next, at opposite ends of the box. The two Swedish ivies should be positioned next, followed by the two geraniums. Finally fill in with the two lobelias.

6. Carefully settle the compost around the plants and level it just below the rim of the window box. Water.

MAINTENANCE

Water regularly, at least once a day and more often in hot weather. Feed twice a week. Regularly tidy the plants.

Gold Splash

NO SINGLE FLOWER *steals the limelight here, but the bright yellow variegations of the pick-a-back plant's foliage draw the eyes and hold the composition together. It seems to hold the colours of the other plants together in an attractive bouquet. There is a wide variation in the shades used, and because most of the plants are trailing varieties, they will pop up throughout the display, fusing colours into a satisfying whole. The box would, perhaps, be sympathetic if it were a more neutral colour.*

INGREDIENTS

2 variegated pick-a-back plants (*Tolmiea menziesii* 'Taff's Gold') **(A)**
1 magenta trailing petunia (*Petunia* 'Bright Pink Surfinia') **(B)**
1 mauve trailing petunia (*Petunia* 'Lilac Super Cascade') **(C)**
2 purple ivy-leaved geraniums (*Pelargonium* 'Lilac Mini Cascade') **(D)**
2 red ivy-leaved geraniums (*Pelargonium* 'Red Mini Cascade') **(E)**
1 pink ivy-leaved geranium (*Pelargonium*' Rose Mini Cascade') **(F)**
3 blue trailing lobelias (*Lobelia* 'Blue Wave') **(G)**

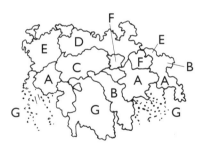

CONTAINER

Wooden window box, painted, with inner plastic container
90cm (36in) long; 20cm (8in) wide; 20cm (8in) deep

MATERIALS

Pieces of old pottery or broken tiles
2.5cm (1in) layer of gravel
General potting compost to fill container

POSITION

This display can be in full sun or in a position that gets sun during most of the day.

PLANTING

1. Because most of the plants used here are frost tender it is best to plant it in early summer, except in warmer areas where it can be prepared earlier.

2. Cover the drainage holes with pieces of pottery so that excess water can drain away but gravel will not trickle out.

3. Add a 2.5cm (1in) layer of gravel or small stones in the bottom of the box to aid the drainage.

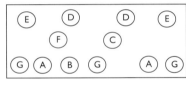

4. Fill the window box with a good, general potting compost.

5. Start by planting the two purple and two red geraniums in a row at the back of the box, the red ones at the ends. Next, position the two variegated pick-a-back plants towards the front of the box. The pink geranium can be planted now, followed by the two petunias – be careful not to break the petunias' brittle stems. Finally, tuck in the three trailing lobelias.

6. Firm down the compost around the plants and level the surface just below the rim of the box.

7. Water.

MAINTENANCE

Water once a day – more often in hot weather – and feed twice a week. Deadhead regularly.

Foliage Effect

*T*HIS WINDOW BOX *is planted entirely for foliage effect, and it is the interplay of the various colours, textures and shapes of the leaves that gives it its impact. These are nearly all tender plants that are more usually seen on the inside of the window rather than the outside, but they are all perfectly happy in the open as long as the weather is not too cold or windy. Any flower stems that appear should be pinched out to preserve the foliage effect.*

INGREDIENTS

1 bronze-leaved coleus (*Coleus blumei*) **(A)**
2 spider plants (*Chlorophytum comosum* 'Vittatum') **(B)**
2 variegated geraniums (*Pelargonium* 'Lady Plymouth') **(C)**
2 variegated pick-a-back plants (*Tolmiea menziesii* 'Taff's Gold') **(D)**
2 emerald ferns (*Asparagus densiflorus* 'Sprengeri') **(E)**
2 tradescantias (*Tradescantia fluminensis* 'Albovittata') **(F)**
2 variegated ivies (*Hedera helix* 'Glacier') **(G)**

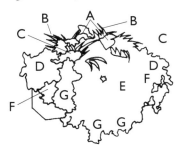

CONTAINER

Wooden window box, painted white, with plastic inner container
90cm (36in) long; 20cm (8in) wide; 20cm (8in) deep

MATERIALS

Pieces of broken pots or tiles
2.5cm (1in) layer of gravel or small stones
General potting compost to fill container

POSITION

Any position that is not too shady. Protect from strong winds.

PLANTING

1. The arrangement can be prepared under glass in spring so that it has filled out by the time it is put out in early summer, or it can be made up outside after the last frosts are over.

2. Cover the drainage holes in the bottom of the box with pieces of old pottery so that excess water can drain away but compost and gravel cannot fall through.

3. Cover the bottom of the box with a 2.5cm (1in) layer of gravel or small stones to improve the drainage.

4. Fill the window box with a general potting compost.

5. Start by planting the coleus towards the back in the middle of the box. As you add the other plants, take care not do damage the leaves of the coleus. Next plant the spider plants, geraniums and the pick-a-back plants, keeping them tightly packed together. In the centre plant the two asparagus ferns, and then tuck in the ivies and tradescantias.

6. This is a tightly planted box so it is not easy to firm down the compost. Tap the box sharply on a table or the ground a few times to settle the compost.

7. Water carefully.

MAINTENANCE

Water at least daily and feed every two days. Keep tidy.

Lobelia Sea

*T*HIS IS A *simple yet effective display, using a surprisingly small number of different varieties. There are, in fact, only three different types, although at first glance there appears to be more. Across the top is a band of zonal geraniums, providing the excitement of bright colours. Below this is a sea of blue lobelias, through which weave strands of lime green helichrysum foliage, almost like foam on the crest of a wave. Although this is a simple display, it is long lasting.*

INGREDIENTS

3 zonal geraniums (*Pelargonium* 'Sophie Dumaresque') **(A)**
2 golden helichrysums (*Helichrysum petiolare* 'Limelight') **(B)**
8 blue lobelias (*Lobelia* 'Blue Wave') **(C)**

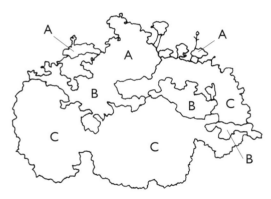

CONTAINER

Wooden window box
90cm (36in) long; 20cm (8in) wide; 20cm (8in) deep

MATERIALS

Pieces of old pottery or broken tiles
2.5cm (1in) layer of gravel
General potting compost to fill container

POSITION

This display can be in full sun or partial shade.

PLANTING

1. Early summer is the best time to plant up this container. Wait until the threat of frosts is passed before putting it out.

2. Cover the drainage holes with pieces of old pottery or broken tile so that excess water can drain away but the gravel and compost cannot be washed away.

3. Cover the bottom of the container with a layer of grit to help with the drainage.

4. Loosely fill the container with a general potting compost.

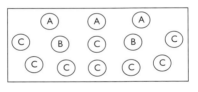

5. Plant the three geraniums in a row towards the back. Plant the helichrysums in front of these, a little forwards of the middle line, then fill in the gaps with the lobelias, which can be planted tight against the front of the box so that they are encouraged to trail over the edge.

6. Press down the compost between the plants and smooth over the surface, which should be just below the rim of the window box.

7. Water.

MAINTENANCE

Water regularly but gently so that the lobelias are not crushed down and spoiled. Feed once every 10 days. Remove any dead flowerheads as they appear.

Contrasting Reds

*I*T IS POSSIBLE *to get away with colour schemes in window boxes that would raise eyebrows if they were used in a border. Here the bright scarlet reds and the rich purple reds go together very effectively, but it is doubtful if they could be used elsewhere. The star performer is the flame-coloured begonia, which is ringed by a skirt of mimulus of a similar colour. This, in turn, is surrounded by the rich purples and deep blues of the petunias and the lobelias. With luck, the box will be covered with plants, so you can use any type of window box, including plastic.*

INGREDIENTS

1 scarlet begonia (*Begonia* × *tuberhybrida*) **(A)**
3 rich purple petunias (*Petunia* 'Purple Surfinia') **(B)**
4 scarlet mimulus (*Mimulus*) **(C)**
2 blue lobelias (*Lobelia* 'Blue Wave') **(D)**

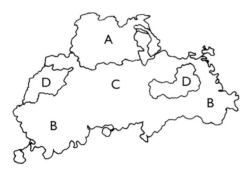

CONTAINER

Wooden window box
60cm (24in) long; 15cm (6in) wide; 15cm (6in) deep

MATERIALS

Pieces of broken pottery or old roof tiles
2.5cm (1in) layer of gravel
Lime-free (ericaceous) compost to fill container

POSITION

A warm sunny position, away from direct rainfall would be the best position.

PLANTING

1. As with so many summer window boxes, the best time to plant is early summer, after the threat of frost has passed.

2. Cover the drainage holes with broken pieces of pottery. These will act as a filter and prevent the contents of the box being washed out.

3. The bottom of the window box should be covered with gravel to aid good drainage.

4. Fill the box with compost. Use a lime-free mixture because begonias prefer slightly acid conditions.

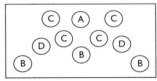

5. Plant the begonia in the centre but towards the back of the box. Place the four mimulus in a semicircle around this. Next plant the three petunias, being careful not to break their fragile stems. The two blue lobelias fill the gaps between the two outer petunias and the ring of mimulus.

6. Gently firm the compost around the plants, and level the surface by adding or removing compost so that it is about 2.5cm (1in) below the edge of the window box.

7. Water.

MAINTENANCE

Water at least once a day and more often in hot weather. Feed twice a week. Remove the dead flowers, particularly from the mimulus and petunias, as they occur.

Red, Yellow and Green

*R*ED FLOWERS ALWAYS *look good when set off against green foliage, but here they have been mixed with golden-variegated leaves, which creates a very sunny effect. This is a display that would cheer up the dullest of days. The key element is the begonias whose scarlet petals are beautifully illuminated by the golden boss of stamens in their centre. The duller red of the geraniums gives a top edge to the display without drawing the eye from the more exciting centre part.*

INGREDIENTS

3 scarlet begonias (*Begonia × tuberhybrida* 'Flamboyant') **(A)**
2 red mini-geraniums (*Pelargonium* 'Blakesdorf') **(B)**
3 variegated geraniums (*Pelargonium crispum* 'Variegatum') **(C)**
4 variegated ivies (*Hedera helix* 'Kolibri') **(D)**

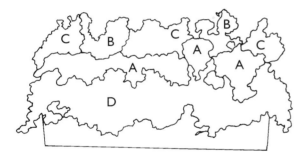

CONTAINER

Wooden window box
90cm (36in) wide; 20cm (8in) wide; 20cm (8in) deep

MATERIALS

Pieces of old pottery or broken roof tiles or slates
2.5cm (1in) layer of gravel
Lime-free (ericaceous) compost to fill container

POSITION

A sunny position is to be preferred but the box should not
get the midday sun or get too hot.

PLANTING

1. This container should be planted in late spring or early summer, once the threat of frost has passed.

2. Cover the drainage holes with pieces of pottery or tile, so that water can freely pass through but gravel and compost cannot trickle out.

3. Add a drainage layer of about 2.5cm (1in) of gravel in the bottom of the box.

4. Loosely fill the container with a compost. This should be lime-free because begonias prefer acidic conditions.

5. Start by planting the row of geraniums at the rear of the window box, alternating the variegated and flowering forms. In front of these plant the three begonias, equally spaced across the front half of the box. Finally tuck in the ivies.

6. Firm down the compost around the plants and top up with more compost if necessary to bring the final level about 2.5cm (1in) below the top of the box.

7. Arrange the trailing stems of the ivy so that they fall naturally and at the same time cover the front of the box.

8. Water.

MAINTENANCE

Water at least once a day during hot weather and feed once a week.

Summer Snow

THE BRILLIANT WHITE band of petunias sits above the brighter coloured plants like a band of summer snow. They would totally dominate the scene, suppressing the other colours, if it were not for the other touches of white throughout the box. If you wanted a more subdued effect, you could use darker coloured petunias. This looks as if it is a complicated display, but it is made up of plants that are easy to obtain or grow yourself, and it should also be easy to look after.

INGREDIENTS

4 white petunias (*Petunia* 'White Falcon') **(A)**
3 blue verbenas (*Verbena* 'Amethyst') **(B)**
2 white marguerites (*Argyranthemum frutescens*) **(C)**
3 mixed pansies (*Viola* 'Universal Mixture') **(D)**
2 pink verbenas (*Verbena* 'Sissinghurst') **(E)**
3 blue lobelias (*Lobelia* 'Blue Wave') **(F)**
1 white viola (*Viola* 'Little David') **(G)**
3 white alyssums (*Alyssum* 'Snow Carpet') **(H)**

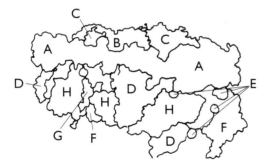

CONTAINER

Wooden window box, painted black
90cm (36in); 20cm (8in) wide; 20cm (8in) deep

MATERIALS

Pieces of broken pots or tiles
2.5cm (1in) layer of gravel or small stones
General potting compost to fill container
Water-retaining granules

POSITION

A sunny, but not too hot, position is best.

PLANTING

1. Plant this window box during late spring or early summer, but not before the threat of frosts has passed.

2. Cover the drainage holes with crocks to allow water to pass through but to prevent the compost from falling out.

3. Cover the bottom of the box with a 2.5cm (1in) layer of gravel or small stones to improve the drainage.

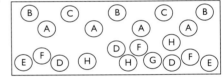

4. Mix the water-retaining granules with the compost and fill the window box with the mixture.

5. Start at the back with the blue verbenas and the marguerites. Do not plant them too far forwards because there are a lot of plants to pack in. Next put in the petunias, being careful not to break their brittle stems. Plant the pink verbenas at the ends of the box and space out the pansies and viola. Fill in the spaces with the alyssums and lobelias.

6. Firm down the compost and level it so that the surface is about 2.5cm (1in) below the top of the box. Water.

MAINTENANCE

Never let the compost dry out – the water-retaining granules should help. Feed twice a week. Remove any dead flowers.

Summer Mixture

*T*HIS IS A *cheerful mixture of bedding plants, such as can be obtained from any garden centre. It is easy to put together and to maintain. The lobelias provides the unifying factor, while the busy lizzies, petunias, fuchsia and geraniums provide the colour. The display has a positive background in the form of three young conifers, but these can be omitted if they are likely to darken the room too much or if you wish to see the window box from indoors.*

INGREDIENTS

3 young conifers (*Chamaecyparis*) **(A)**
1 fuchsia (*Fuchsia* 'Jack Acland') **(B)**
3 busy lizzies (*Impatiens* 'Novette Series') **(C)**
2 purple petunias (*Petunia* 'Deep Purple') **(D)**
1 trailing geranium (*Pelargonium* 'Rouletta') **(E)**
1 scarlet zonal geranium (*Pelargonium* 'Victorious') **(F)**
1 rose-pink zonal geranium (*Pelargonium* 'Lady Folkestone') **(G)**
4 blue lobelias (*Lobelia* 'Blue Wave') **(H)**

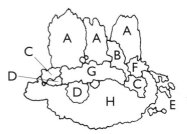

CONTAINER

Wooden or plastic window box, painted white
75cm (30in) long; 20cm (8in) wide; 20cm (8in) deep

MATERIALS

Pieces of broken pots or tiles
2.5cm (1in) layer of gravel or small stones
General potting compost to fill container

POSITION

A sunny position that does not get too hot.

PLANTING

1. Plant this container in early summer, when it is safe to put these tender plants outside.

2. Cover the drainage holes with pieces of old pottery, so that water can drain away but compost will not be washed away.

3. Cover the bottom 2.5cm (1in) of the box with gravel to improve the drainage.

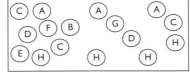

4. Fill the container with a general potting compost.

5. Plant the three conifers as close to the back of the window box as possible. If the sill is wide enough, consider planting them in individual pots and standing them behind the box. Next plant the fuchsia, followed by the three geraniums. These should be followed by the busy lizzies and the petunias. Finally fill in the gaps along the front with the lobelias.

6. Gently firm the compost around the plants and level the surface so that it is just below the rim of the window box.

7. Water.

MAINTENANCE

Water regularly – at least once a day and more often in hot weather. Feed twice a week with a liquid feed added to the water. The display will quickly look untidy if the dead flowers are not regularly removed. The conifers can be reused, but they will eventually grow too large for further use.

Something Simple

*T*HIS IS ANOTHER *simple display, consisting of only two different types of plants, lobelias and busy lizzies. Mixed colours of both are used, and the choice of colours and their disposition within the arrangement rests with the gardener. Because of its simplicity this is a good choice for beginners, but, when it is done well, it will give as much satisfaction as a more complicated design. If you use a plastic container, make sure it is ribbed for both decoration and strength.*

INGREDIENTS

3 mixed busy lizzies (*Impatiens* 'Daydream Mixed') **(A)**
4 mixed lobelias (*Lobelia* 'Cascade Mixed') **(B)**

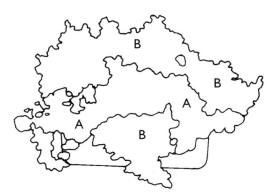

CONTAINER

Plastic window box
30cm (12in) long; 10cm (4in) wide; 10cm (4in) deep

MATERIALS

Pieces of old pottery or tiles
2.5cm (1in) layer of gravel or small stones
General potting compost to fill container

POSITION

Although these plants will tolerate some sun, they will do best if they are shaded during the hottest part of the day.

PLANTING

1. Plant out in the first week of early summer. If it is earlier, the plants may be killed by late frosts.

2. Cover the drainage holes with crocks to prevent the compost from falling out, while still allowing the excess water to drain away.

3. Put a 2.5cm (1in) layer of gravel in the bottom of the box to prevent the compost becoming waterlogged.

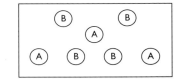

4. Fill the box with a general potting compost.

5. This is only a small box and the plants will soon spread to form a mass of blooms that seem to have little relationship to where they are rooted. Some kind of order can be kept for a while by planting the three busy lizzies as shown on the plan and filling in the gaps with the lobelias.

6. Gently tamp down the compost around the plants and smooth the surface of the compost so that the final level is just below the rim of the box.

7. Water.

MAINTENANCE

These are quite thirsty plants, so keep the compost moist by watering once a day. Feed every week, but do not overfeed or they will become too large for the container. Trim off dead flowers and stems regularly.

Versatile Framework

*T*HIS IS A NARROW *trough, but it contains a wide variety of plants that combine together to make an attractive display. The bright colours of the flowers and the dark shiny foliage of the begonias provide most of the interest, while the trailing ivies in the front of the box and spotted laurels at the back create the framework. The geraniums and lobelias add the finishing touches. Any number of designs with other flowers could be made around the structure provided by the box and laurels.*

INGREDIENTS

1 box (*Buxus sempervirens*) **(A)**
1 white begonia (*Begonia semperflorens*) **(B)**
3 scarlet begonias (*Begonia semperflorens*) **(C)**
4 pink zonal geraniums (*Pelargonium* 'Caledonia') **(D)**
2 spotted laurels (*Aucuba japonica* 'Gold Dust') **(E)**
2 variegated ivies (*Hedera helix* 'Eva') **(F)**
2 blue lobelias (*Lobelia* 'Blue Wave') **(G)**

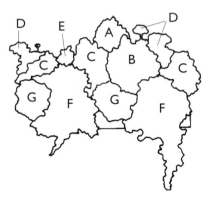

CONTAINER

Moulded plastic window box, the same colour as the window-frame
75cm (30in) long; 15cm (6in) wide; 20cm (8in) deep

MATERIALS

Pieces of broken pots or tiles
2.5cm (1in) layer of gravel or small stones
Lime-free (ericaceous) compost to fill container

POSITION

Place in a generally sunny spot but away from the real heat of the midday sun if possible.

PLANTING

1. Plant up this box in late spring or early summer, once the frosts have passed.

2. Place pieces of pottery over the drainage holes so that excess water can drain through but the gravel and compost are held back.

3. Cover the bottom of the box with a 2.5cm (1in) layer of gravel to improve drainage.

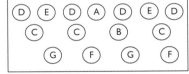

4. Fill the box with a lime-free compost because begonias prefer acidic conditions.

5. Begin by planting the shrubs, then the geraniums. Keep all these well to the back of the box. Next plant the begonias. Finally, the ivies and lobelias are planted alternately in the front of the box so that they trail over the edge.

6. Firm down the compost around the plants and level the surface so that it is about 2.5cm (1in) below the rim of the box. Water.

MAINTENANCE

Water at least once a day and feed once a week. Deadhead as required, trimming back the lobelias if they get straggly.

Full Colour

*T*HIS COLOURFUL WINDOW *box is composed of commonly available plants that can be obtained at any garden centre or nursery, and there is nothing special about the design – it is just a collection of geraniums and other plants making a colourful spectacle of themselves. However, the packed nature of the box and combination of forms ensure that there is always something of interest to look at. The petunia seems to be a bit lost, but it will come into its own when it is in full flower and spreads right across the box.*

INGREDIENTS

4 bright red zonal geraniums (*Pelargonium* 'Electra') **(A)**
3 rose pink ivy-leaved geraniums (*Pelargonium* 'Amethyst') **(B)**
1 pink petunia (*Petunia* 'Falcon Salmon') **(C)**
2 pinkish-red and violet fuchsias (*Fuchsia* 'Border Queen') **(D)**
2 pinkish-red and white fuchsias (*Fuchsia* 'Cloverdale Pearl') **(E)**
4 blue lobelias (*Lobelia* 'Blue Wave') **(F)**

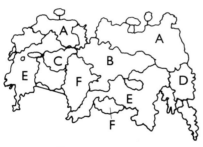

CONTAINER

Wooden window box, painted black
90cm (36in) long; 20cm (8in) wide; 20cm (8in) deep

MATERIALS

Pieces of broken pots or tiles
2.5cm (1in) layer of gravel or small stones
General potting compost to fill container
Water-retaining granules

POSITION

A sunny window-sill is best, but one shaded from the hot midday sun.

PLANTING

1. All the plants in this display are tender, so do not make the box up until frosts have finished.

2. Cover the drainage holes with the pieces of old tile or pottery so that excess water can drain away but the compost and gravel cannot block the holes.

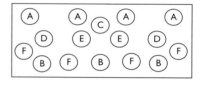

3. Fill the base of the box with about 2.5cm (1in) of gravel or small stones to improve the drainage.

4. Fill the window box with a mixture of general potting compost and water-retaining granules.

5. Starting at the back, plant the four zonal geraniums, leaving extra space in the centre of the box. Just forwards of this gap, plant the petunia. Next plant the four fuchsias as shown on the plan. The trailing geraniums can be planted and finally the lobelias should be tucked in. All the plants, apart from the zonal geraniums, should be allowed to trail over the edges of the box.

6. Firm down the compost and level the surface to about 2.5cm (1in) below the rim of the box.

7. Water.

MAINTENANCE

Water regularly and feed twice a week. Deadhead when necessary.

Mount Vesuvius

A LITTLE IMAGINATION *transforms what could be a simple box of busy lizzies into an exciting spectacle, with the red-hot busy lizzies erupting into a fountain of green leaves. One of the beauties of this display is that, although it is a large one, covering quite a lot of the window, the slender, arching leaves of the cordyline allow light to enter the room beyond, and the curious can still see out.*

INGREDIENTS

1 spiky cordyline (*Cordyline australis*) **(A)**
1 pale pink busy lizzie (*Impatiens*) **(B)**
1 rose-pink busy lizzie (*Impatiens*) **(C)**
4 bright red busy lizzies (*Impatiens*) **(D)**
2 variegated ivies (*Hedera helix* 'Glacier') **(E)**
2 dwarf hypericums (*Hypericum olympicum*) **(F)**

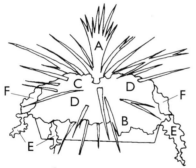

CONTAINER

Terracotta window box
45cm (18in) long; 15cm (6in) wide; 15cm (6in) deep

MATERIALS

Pieces of broken pottery or tiles
2.5cm (1in) layer of gravel or small stones
General potting compost to fill container

POSITION

Although this display will look best in a sunny position, it should not be too hot, so avoid midday sun. Avoid windy sites.

PLANTING

1. The best time to plant this container is in late spring or early summer, when all threat of frosts is safely over.

2. Place pieces of broken pottery over the holes so that they do not become blocked by gravel or compost.

3. To help with free drainage, fill the bottom 2.5cm (1in) of the box with gravel.

4. Fill the window box with a general potting compost.

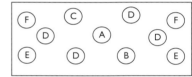

5. Start by planting the cordyline in the centre of the box. So that you damage neither the plant nor yourself while planting the rest of the box, gently ease all the leaves up into a column and loosely tie them together. Put the pink busy lizzies in place and fill in with the red ones. If you prefer, they can all be red. Finally tuck a hypericum and one ivy into each end.

6. Firm down the compost between the plants and level the surface so that it is about 2.5cm (1in) below the rim.

7. Release the leaves of the cordyline and arrange the trailing stems of the other plants to look natural.

8. Water.

MAINTENANCE

Water regularly but be careful not to overdo it, the soil should not become waterlogged. Feed once a week. Remove dead flowers and any straggly stems.

Silver and Purple

*T*HIS IS A *splendid window box with a lovely mixture of colours that not only combine well together but also suit the white walls of the house. In spite of all its luxurious appearance, this box is easy to create, and all the ingredients are readily available. Tucked in at the back are two dwarf conifers. These can be omitted because they are hidden by the other plants once the box gets into full growth. A similar box could be created with pink flowers.*

INGREDIENTS

2 young conifers (*Chamaecyparis*) **(A)**
2 helichrysums (*Helichrysum petiolare*) **(B)**
4 purple petunias (*Petunia* 'Blue Joy') **(C)**
4 lobelias (*Lobelia* 'Blue Wave') **(D)**
2 pink verbenas (*Verbena* 'Silver Anne') **(E)**

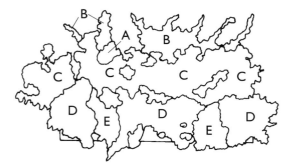

CONTAINER

Wooden window box, painted white
90cm (36in) long; 15cm (6in) wide; 15cm (6in) deep

MATERIALS

Pieces of broken pottery or old bits of tile
2.5cm (1in) layer of gravel
General potting compost to fill container

POSITION

A sunny window-sill protected from strong winds or draughts.

PLANTING

1. Do not make a start on this window box until the beginning of summer, when all frosts are over.

2. Cover the drainage holes pieces of pottery so that the compost cannot clog them but water can drain freely away.

3. Fill the bottom of the box with about 2.5cm (1in) of gravel to improve drainage.

4. Fill the rest of the box with a general potting compost.

5. Start by planting the two conifers in the back corners of the box. Between them set the two helichrysums and plant an equally 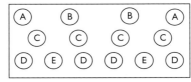 spaced row of petunias, roughly along the middle line of the box. Finally, plant the lobelias and verbenas along the front of the box, allowing them to trail over the edge.

6. Firm the compost around the plants and top up so that the final level is about 2.5cm (1in) below the rim of the box.

7. Tease out the stems of the helichrysums so that they weave through the other plants.

8. Water.

MAINTENANCE

Water regularly – at least once a day in summer – and feed twice a week with a liquid feed. Remove dead and dying flowers as they appear, or the box will quickly look untidy.

Summer Bouquet

A WINDOW BOX of such profusion is little less than perfection – it becomes a celebration of summer. Not only is it filled with rich, vibrant colours, but there are all manner of shapes and textures. It has a fullness about it that suggests plenty and opulence, and yet it is composed of very basic elements, mainly a mixture of different coloured petunias and geraniums, plants that anyone can obtain and grow. The dominance of red, with just touches of purple and white, makes it easy for even the most inartistic person to put together without causing colour clashes.

INGREDIENTS

1 bright green young conifer (*Thuja orientalis*) **(A)**
3 scarlet geraniums (*Pelargonium* 'Fritz Anders') **(B)**
1 variegated hebe (*Hebe × franciscana* 'Variegata') **(C)**
2 pink geraniums (*Pelargonium* 'Ice Crystal') **(D)**
6 mixed colour petunias (*Petunia*) **(E)**
2 fuchsias (*Fuchsia* 'General Monk') **(F)**
2 helichrysums (*Helichrysum petiolare*) **(G)**
3 blue lobelias (*Lobelia* 'Blue Wave') **(H)**

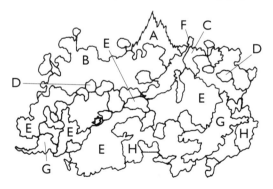

CONTAINER

Wooden window box, painted white
90cm (36in) long; 20cm (8in) wide; 20cm (8in) deep

MATERIALS

Pieces of old tile or pottery
2.5cm (1in) layer of gravel or small stones
General potting compost to fill container
Water-retaining granules

POSITION

A sunny window-sill, protected from strong winds and draughts.

PLANTING

1. Early summer is the best time for planting this window box.

2. Cover the drainage holes with pieces of old pottery to prevent the compost and gravel from falling through, yet allowing excess water to drain away.

3. Add a 2.5cm (1in) layer of gravel or small stones in the bottom of the box to improve the drainage.

4. Fill the container with a good general potting compost that has had some water-retaining granules mixed into it.

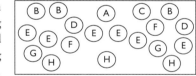

5. This is a very full container, so set the plants close together. Begin by planting the conifer and the hebe close to the back. Follow these with the geraniums. The petunias are planted next – be careful not to break their brittle stems. The fuchsias and helichrysums are planted next, and finally the lobelias are tucked in.

6. Water.

MAINTENANCE

Water at least once a day – more often in hot weather – and feed twice a week. Deadhead regularly.

Molten Gold

M OST SUMMER WINDOW *boxes seem to rely on various shades of red for their colour, so it comes almost as a shock to have clumps of molten gold introduced into a scheme. This display of soft pinks and whites has suddenly been enlivened by the introduction of the deep yellow pansies, which immediately draw the eye. This is a nicely flowing window box with plenty of foliage against which the colours are shown to their best advantage.*

INGREDIENTS

3 helichrysums (*Helichrysum petiolare*) **(A)**
2 white busy lizzies (*Impatiens*) **(B)**
2 pink busy lizzies (*Impatiens*) **(C)**
2 pink verbenas (*Verbena* 'Sissinghurst') **(D)**
3 yellow pansies (*Viola* 'Universal Yellow') **(E)**
2 trailing geraniums (*Pelargonium* 'Ice Crystal') **(F)**
3 variegated ivies (*Hedera helix* 'Glacier') **(G)**
4 white alyssums (*Alyssum* ' Snow Carpet') **(H)**

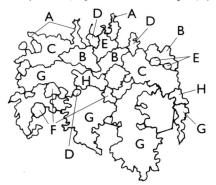

CONTAINER

Wooden window box, painted white
90cm (36in) long; 20cm (8in) wide; 20cm (8in) deep

MATERIALS

Pieces of broken pottery or pieces of tile
2.5cm (1in) layer of gravel or small stones
General potting compost to fill container
Water-retaining granules

POSITION

A sunny, not too windy, position is needed.

PLANTING

1. Early summer is the best time to prepare this display.

2. Place broken pottery over the drainage holes so that excess water can pass through but compost is held back.

3. Cover the bottom 2.5cm (1in) of the box with gravel to improve drainage.

4. Mix water-retaining granules with the compost and fill the box with the mixture.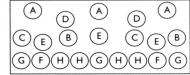

5. Start at the back of the box by planting the helichrysums. Next set the verbenas just in front of these and the four busy lizzies in front of the verbenas, alternating the pink and white. Follow this with the pansies and finally the front row of ivies, trailing geraniums and alyssums.

6. If you can, firm down the compost between the plants and level the surface at about 2.5cm (1in) below the rim of the box. If the box is not fixed at this stage, tap it sharply on a table or on the ground a few times to settle the compost.

7. Water.

MAINTENANCE

Water at least once a day and feed twice a week. Deadhead and tidy regularly.

Flaming Passion

*N*ASTURTIUMS MAKE EXCELLENT *window box plants. They are not only colourful and cheerful, but they also flower over a long period. Although there are more shrubby plants available now, the old-fashioned trailing varieties have a lot going for them, and the flame red flowers have the greatest impact in a display. Here, the colour of the nasturtiums is nicely balanced by the other colours in the top corner, especially the white, while the blues of the lobelias are a perfect foil to their trailing stems.*

INGREDIENTS

2 fuchsias (*Fuchsia* 'Tennessee Waltz') **(A)**
1 white zonal geranium (*Pelargonium* 'Highfield's White') **(B)**
3 mixed coloured petunias (*Petunia* 'Polo Mixed') **(C)**
2 nasturtiums (*Tropaeolum majus*) **(D)**
4 mixed lobelias (*Lobelia* 'Cascade') **(E)**

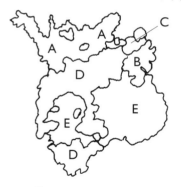

CONTAINER

Wooden window box, painted black
45cm (18in) long; 20cm (8in) wide; 20cm (8in) deep

MATERIALS

Pieces of old tiles or pottery
2.5cm (1in) layer of gravel or small stones
General potting compost to fill container

POSITION

A sunny window-sill, protected from strong winds and
draughts, would be best for this trailing display.

PLANTING

1. Early summer, after frosts have departed, is the best time to plant this window box.

2. Cover the holes in the base of the box with pieces of pottery so that excess water can drain away freely, but the compost and gravel are kept clear of the holes.

3. Cover the bottom of the box with a 2.5cm (1in) layer of gravel to improve drainage.

4. Fill the box with a general potting compost.

5. Plant the fuchsias first, followed by the white geranium. Next plant the three petunias. Any colours can be  included, but the purple enriches the display while the reds complement the nasturtiums. The nasturtiums can now be planted. Be careful with both the petunias and the nasturtiums because both have brittle stems. Finally, plant the trailing lobelias along the front edge.

6. Firm down the compost between the plants and level the surface so that it is about 2.5cm (1in) below the rim .

7. Arrange the trailing stems so that they look natural.

8. Water.

MAINTENANCE

Water regularly – at least once a day and more frequently during hot weather – and apply a liquid feed twice a week.

Golden Rays

*T*HE MAIN POINT *of interest in this window box is the yellow of the violas, but their colour is also delightfully echoed in the leaves of the helichrysums and pick-a-back plants. The asarinas, a relative of the antirrhinum, provide the dark background foliage as well as further touches of yellow when the snapdragon-like flowers begin to appear. This is a trailing plant that is not often seen in window boxes but is well worth considering.*

INGREDIENTS

3 yellow marguerites (*Argyranthemum frutescens* 'Jamaica Primrose') **(A)**
5 yellow violas (*Viola* 'David Wheldon') **(B)**
3 golden helichrysums (*Helichrysum petiolare* 'Limelight') **(C)**
4 asarinas (*Asarina procumbens*) **(D)**
2 variegated pick-a-back plants (*Tolmiea menziesii* 'Taff's Gold')

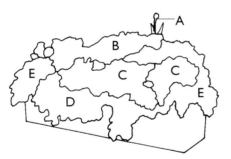

CONTAINER

Wooden window box, painted white
90cm (36in) long; 20cm (8in) wide; 20cm (8in) deep

MATERIALS

Pieces of broken pottery or bits of old tiles
2.5cm (1in) layer of gravel or small stones
General potting compost to fill container

POSITION

A sunny, but not too warm position or a lightly shaded place will suit this arrangement.

PLANTING

1. Late spring or early summer would be the best time to prepare this display.

2. Cover the drainage holes with pieces of broken pottery so that the compost and gravel will not fall through and prevent the free drainage of excess water.

3. Improve the drainage by covering the bottom of the box with a 2.5cm (1in) layer of gravel or small stones.

4. Fill the box with a general potting compost.

5. The three yellow marguerites should be planted first, at the back of the box. These will bloom later in the season and extend the

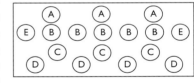

flowering period of the display. Plant the violas in a row, with the pick-a-back plants at either end. The helichrysums follow, with the asarinas being planted last, along the front of the box so that they can trail over the edge.

6. Smooth over the surface of the compost after firming it down around the plants. Level it off at about 2.5cm (1in) below the top of the box.

7. Water.

MAINTENANCE

Water every day, but do not allow the compost to become waterlogged. Feed once a week. Remove any dead viola blooms and cut back the plants if they become too straggly.

A Dash of Everything

*T*HIS DISPLAY SEEMS *to have a dash of all the usual window box plants in it – plus a cordyline to add something different. Indeed, the cordyline is the centrepiece of this display, giving it height and structure without obscuring the window. The other plants provide a joyful mixture of colours that will give pleasure throughout summer and well into autumn. House plants have been happily mixed with the more usual garden plants.*

INGREDIENTS

1 cordyline (*Cordyline australis*) **(A)**
2 spider plants (*Chlorophytum comosum* 'Vittatum') **(B)**
2 coleus (*Coleus blumei*) **(C)**
6 begonias (*Begonia semperflorens*) **(D)**
1 miniature zonal geranium (*Pelargonium* 'Candy') **(E)**
2 trailing geraniums (*Pelargonium* 'Amethyst') **(F)**
4 French marigolds (*Tagetes* 'Goldfinch') **(G)**
4 blue lobelias (*Lobelia* 'Blue Gown') **(H)**
3 white heathers (*Calluna vulgaris* 'Anthony Davis') **(I)**
2 trailing ivies (*Hedera helix* 'Glacier') **(J)**

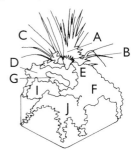

CONTAINER

Wooden window box, painted white
90cm (36in) long; 20cm (8in) wide; 20cm (8in) deep

MATERIALS

Pieces of broken pottery or pieces of old slate
2.5cm (1in) layer of gravel
Lime-free (ericaceous) compost to fill container
Water-retaining granules

POSITION

Site this box in any sunny position.

PLANTING

1. Prepare this window box in either late spring or early summer, once the last frosts have finished.

2. Cover the drainage holes with broken pottery so that water can get out, but compost and gravel are retained in the box.

3. Fill the bottom of the box with about 2.5cm (1in) of gravel or small stones to improve the drainage.

4. Fill the window box with lime-free compost because the heathers prefer acidic conditions. Mix some water-retaining granules with it.

5. The cordyline is the first plant to set in place. Gently pull all the leaves up into a column and tie them together so that they will not get damaged. 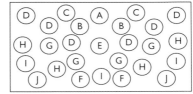 Work outwards in a semicircle, planting the various plants as indicated on the plan. Press down the compost as you work.

6. Release the cordyline leaves and water the box.

MAINTENANCE

Water at least once a day and feed twice a week. Remove any dead flowers and keep tidy or this box will soon look tatty.

Single Subjects

*S*OME OF THE *simplest window boxes you can have are created with a single subject. The plant should be carefully chosen, or it may look bland and rather boring. Here, the choice of a bright orange begonia is perfect. Not only does it provide the right balance of flower to foliage, but it fits in perfectly with the old terracotta window box. The container is important, because it can be seen and plays a part in the overall effect.*

INGREDIENTS

3 begonias (*Begonia* × *tuberhybrida*) **(A)**

ALTERNATIVE INGREDIENTS

2 miniature roses (*Rosa* 'China Doll')
3 rock origanums (*Origanum* 'Kent Beauty')
4 diascias (*Diascia* 'Jack Elliott')

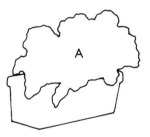

CONTAINER

Terracotta pot
30cm (12in) long; 10cm (4in) wide; 15cm (6in) deep

MATERIALS

Pieces of old pottery or broken roof tiles
2.5cm (1in) layer of gravel
Lime-free (ericaceous) compost to fill container

POSITION

The choice of site will depend on the subject. The begonias will prefer a light but not too hot a position.

PLANTING

1. The time of planting will depend on the subject. A small box like this can be prepared in advance under glass and moved outside when the weather is suitable. Begonias should not be set outside until all threat of frost has passed.

2. So that the gravel and compost do not clog the drainage holes, protect them with a piece of old pottery or tile.

3. Even moisture-loving plants need to have free drainage, so cover the bottom of the box with a layer of at least 2.5cm (1in) of gravel or small stones.

4. Fill the container with a lime-free compost because begonias will not thrive in lime or chalk.

5. Single subjects rarely present a problem with planting. In this case they are in a simple straight line. With bulbs and other plants that might vary in height, plant out after they have reached their full height so that you can arrange them with the tallest in the middle.

6. Always firm down the compost around the plants and level it off so that the surface is about 2.5cm (1in) below the top of the box.

7. Water.

MAINTENANCE

Most plants should never be allowed to dry out and begonias are no exception. Feed once a week.

Herbs A-plenty

*N*OT ALL WINDOW *boxes need be limited to providing a visual display. One practical way of using a box is to grow herbs in it, and when this is done well, it is not only a way of providing herbs for the kitchen but also a way of producing a box that is visually different. On the whole, herbs do not produce colourful flowers — most are interesting for their foliage — but in this display the nasturtiums will soon brighten up the scene.*

INGREDIENTS

1 bay laurel (*Laurus nobilis*) **(A)**
2 fennels (*Foeniculum vulgare*) **(B)**
4 parsley (*Petroselinum crispum*) **(C)**
2 sages (*Salvia officinalis*) **(D)**
2 clumps of chives (*Allium schoenoprasum*) **(E)**
1 variegated thyme (*Thymus* × *citriodorus* 'Bertram Anderson') **(F)**
2 borages (*Borago officinalis*) **(G)**
2 mints (*Mentha spicata*) **(H)**
1 variegated balm (*Melissa officinalis* 'Variegata') **(I)**
1 basil (*Ocimum basilicum*) **(J)**
1 purple basil (*Ocimum basilicum* 'Purpurascens') **(K)**
2 heartsease (*Viola tricolor*) **(L)**
5 variegated nasturtiums (*Tropaeolum majus* 'Alaska') **(M)**
2 thymes (*Thymus serpyllum*) **(N)**

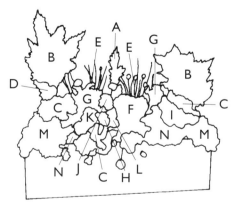

CONTAINER

Wooden window box, painted white
90cm (30in) long; 20cm (8in) wide; 20cm (8in) deep

MATERIALS

Pieces of broken pottery or bits of old roof tiles
2.5cm (1in) layer of gravel
General potting compost to fill container

POSITION

A sunny site is necessary.

PLANTING

1. Prepare the box while the plants are young. Spring would be the best time.

2. Cover the drainage holes with pieces of broken pottery.

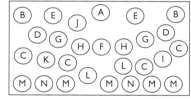

3. Put a 2.5cm (1in) layer of gravel in the bottom of the box to aid drainage. Fill the container with compost.

4. There are, in reality, too many plants here to make a useful herb box, so select the ones you most require and plant them in whatever design you wish. The box as shown will remain pretty for a while and will then need replanting as it becomes overgrown.

5. Make sure that the compost has been gently but firmly pressed down around the plants. Water.

MAINTENANCE

Water daily and feed twice a week. Herbs can become untidy, so cut them back so that they re-shoot with fresh foliage.

Yellow Eyes

*I*N THIS DISPLAY *the eye is inevitably drawn towards the two bight yellow chrysanthemums. These are dwarf forms of the kind usually sold by florists for use indoors as potted plants. Autumn is one of the most difficult times of the year when it comes to providing flower colour, but here is a selection of plants that will help to keep the box interesting up to Christmas as long as the weather is not too severe. If the plants are kept in their original pots they can easily be substituted for others should they begin to wither.*

INGREDIENTS

2 variegated hebes (*Hebe × franciscana* 'Variegata') **(A)**
2 deep purple heathers (*Calluna vulgaris* 'Darkness') **(B)**
1 white heather (*Calluna vulgaris* 'Anthony Davis') **(C)**
2 Christmas cherries (*Solanum capsicastrum*) **(D)**
1 small spotted laurel (*Aucuba japonica* 'Variegata') **(E)**
2 yellow chrysanthemums (*Dendranthema*) **(F)**
2 silver cinerarias (*Senecio cineraria*) **(G)**
4 trailing ivies (*Hedera helix*) **(H)**

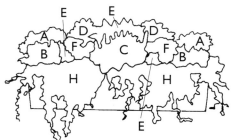

CONTAINER

Wooden window box
75cm (30in) long; 20cm (8in) wide; 20cm (8in) deep

MATERIALS

Pieces of old pottery or broken tile
2.5cm (1in) layer of gravel or small stones
Lime-free (ericaceous) compost to fill container

POSITION

A sunny position is best, but a partially shaded one will do.

PLANTING

1. Plant this up in late summer or when the plants are in flower.

2. Cover the drainage holes with pieces of pottery so that the compost cannot trickle out but excess water can easily drain away.

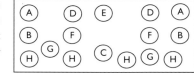

3. Cover the bottom of the window box with a 2.5cm (1in) layer of gravel or small stones.

4. Fill the box with lime-free compost because heathers will not tolerate lime.

5. Plant the spotted laurel in the centre at the back of the box. In each of the two back corners plant a hebe, and half-way between each hebe and the laurel add the two Christmas cherries. Next plant the three heathers with the white one in the centre and the others in the front corners. The cinerarias and the florist's chrysanthemums are planted between them, with the trailing ivies along the front.

6. Smooth over and firm down the compost between the plants and adjust the level until the final surface is just below the rim of the box.

7. Water.

MAINTENANCE

Water regularly, but avoid over-watering in a wet autumn. The plants could be left in their pots, with compost packed among them so that you can quickly swap plants if necessary.

Christmas Cherries

*T*HIS DISPLAY OF *three types of plant could hardly be simpler, yet it is extremely effective. It shows what can be achieved with a little imagination. The three plants involved are brought together from different aspects of the garden to make an extremely attractive picture. The basic ingredient is the Christmas cherries, whose bright orange berries (not edible) immediately take the eye. The purple-leaved bugle forms a perfect edging foil, while the white heathers act almost as bookends. The window box in the illustration was decorated with old bathroom tiles.*

INGREDIENTS

4 Christmas cherries (*Solanum capsicastrum*) **(A)**
4 white heathers (*Erica × darleyensis* 'White Perfection') **(B)**
10 purple-leaved bugles (*Ajuga reptans* 'Atropurpurea') **(C)**

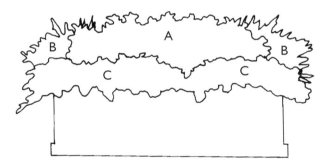

CONTAINER

Wooden window box, painted black
60cm (24in) long; 15cm (6in) wide; 20cm (8in) deep

MATERIALS

Pieces of old pottery or broken tiles
2.5cm (1in) layer of gravel or small stones
General potting compost to fill container

POSITION

A sunny position is preferable, although partial shade would be tolerated.

PLANTING

1. Set out the plants in autumn.

2. Cover the drainage holes with the pieces of old crockery so gravel and compost will not be washed away but excess water can easily drain through the holes.

3. Put a 2.5cm (1in) layer of gravel or small stones in the bottom of the container to improve the drainage.

4. Fill the window box with a general potting compost.

5. Start by planting the four Christmas cherries in a line along the centre of the box, leaving space in the back corners for the heathers. Finally, plant the bugles along the front edge and 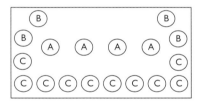 just round the corners to provide an attractive edging.

6. Firm down the compost around the plants and level the surface, which should be about 2.5cm (1in) below the rim of the box.

7. Water.

MAINTENANCE

Do not over-water. The plants need watering only when the compost has almost dried out. Feed once a month. Because the Christmas cherries are tender, the window box must be in a frost-free position or it must be protected when the temperature is likely to drop.

Winter Comfort

*I*N SUMMER *A window box like this would be considered terribly dull, but in midwinter, when there are few flowers around, it will do a great deal to brighten up the façade of a building, giving joy to those both inside and out. The main colour comes from the cyclamen. Some of the heathers have already flowered, but the dead flowers will remain throughout winter. The two ivies, one of which is flushed pink in winter, are a contrast of both form and colour.*

INGREDIENTS

3 red florist's cyclamen (*Cyclamen*) **(A)**
2 white florist's cyclamen (*Cyclamen*) **(B)**
5 young winter-flowering heathers (*Erica lusitanica*) **(C)**
3 variegated ivies (*Hedera helix* 'Eva') **(D)**
2 three-coloured variegated ivies (*Hedera helix* 'Cavendishii') **(E)**

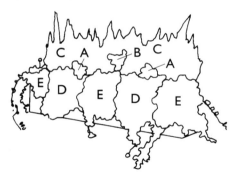

CONTAINER

Wooden window box, painted black
60cm (24in) long; 15cm (6in) wide; 15cm (6in) deep

MATERIALS

Pieces of irregularly shaped stone, broken pots or tiles
2.5cm (1in) layer of gravel or small stones
Lime-free (ericaceous) compost to fill container

POSITION

Sun or partial shade will do, as long as the box is not too dark in winter. Cyclamen are tender, so chose a warm site.

PLANTING

1. Autumn would be a good time to plant this container. Leave gaps so that you can add the cyclamen when they are in flower.

2. Partly cover the drainage holes so that gravel and compost cannot fall out but excess water can drain away.

3. Cover the base of the box with a 2.5cm (1in) layer of gravel or small stones to improve the drainage.

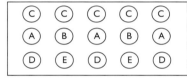

4. Fill the container with a lime-free potting compost because the heathers will not tolerate lime.

5. Begin by planting the heathers, equally spaced, along the back of the box. If they are ready, next plant the cyclamen, so that the tops of their corms are just level with the surface of the compost. Finally, plant the two varieties of ivy alternately along the front so that they can trail over the edge.

6. Firm down the compost between the plants so that the final level is about 2.5cm (1in) below the rim of the box.

7. Water.

MAINTENANCE

Water sparingly in winter and only when the compost dries out. Replace the cyclamen when they have finished flowering or if they are caught by a frost. Bulbs of small daffodils can be included for spring flowering.

Winter Colour

A COLOURFUL WINDOW *box in the middle of winter is difficult to achieve, but here is an extremely good example of what can be done. It is a simple scheme, created from nothing more than florist's cyclamen and violas, yet it works perfectly, providing a colourful display that would be the envy of many even in high summer. The cyclamen are tender, so this arrangement will work only where winters are mild or where the boxes can be protected during cold spells. The window box in the illustration was made to fit within the iron railings.*

INGREDIENTS

5 mixed coloured florist's cyclamens (*Cyclamen*) **(A)**
6 purple violas (*Viola* 'Martin') **(B)**

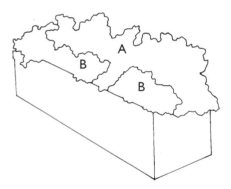

CONTAINER

Wooden window box, painted white
60cm (24in) long; 20cm (8in) wide; 25cm (10in) deep

MATERIALS

Pieces of old pottery or broken roof tiles
2.5cm (1in) layer of gravel or small stones
General potting compost to fill container

POSITION

A sunny position that does not get too hot in winter sunshine is ideal. Cyclamen are tender, so the site should be frost free.

PLANTING

1. Plant this container when you are ready to put it out, growing on the plants in individual pots.

2. Cover the drainage holes with pieces of pottery to prevent them from becoming clogged with compost and to allow excess water to drain away.

3. Place a 2.5cm (1in) layer of gravel or small stones in the bottom of the window box to improve drainage.

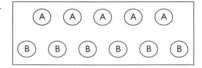

4. Fill the container with a general potting compost.

5. Plant the cyclamen, spacing them evenly along the back half of the container and planting them so that the tops of the corms are level with the surface of the compost. The order you choose will depend on the plants that are available. Plant the violas in front of them. As the season progresses, these will begin to flop over the edge.

6. Firm down the compost and level it off so that the surface is about 2.5cm (1in) below the top of the box.

7. Water.

MAINTENANCE

Water only when the compost begins to dry out. Feed once every 10 days. If the cyclamen finish flowering or get caught by a cold snap, replace them with fresh plants. To make this easier, leave the plants in their pots and plunge the pots into the compost.

Winter Simplicity

*O*NCE AGAIN, THIS *arrangement proves that simple designs are sometimes the most effective. Winter can be a dull time for the gardener, but here, with only three basic ingredients, a very attractive display has been created. Colour, shape and texture, the three basic qualities of garden design, all play their part in an imaginative and pleasing way. The cyclamen, of course, are the plants that catch the eye, but unfortunately these can be grown outside only in warm areas or in the centre of towns.*

INGREDIENTS

4 conical box (*Buxus sempervirens*) **(A)**
5 red florist's cyclamen (*Cyclamen*) **(B)**
4 variegated ivies (*Hedera helix* 'Eva') **(C)**

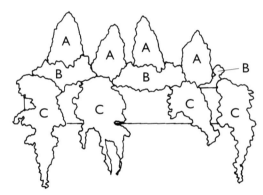

CONTAINERS

2 moulded plastic window boxes
Overall size 150cm (5ft) long; 15cm (6in) wide;
20cm (8in) deep

MATERIALS

Pieces of broken pots or tiles
2.5cm (1in) layer of gravel or small stones
General potting compost to fill container

POSITION

A sunny position is required. It should be warm and frost free unless protection can be given during cold spells.

PLANTING

1. Plant up the window box when the cyclamen come into flower.

2. Cover the drainage holes with bits of pottery so that the gravel and compost do not clog the holes and prevent excess water from draining away.

3. Put a 2.5cm (1in) layer of gravel or small stones in the bottom of the box to improve drainage.

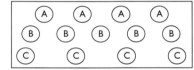

4. Fill the window boxes with a general potting compost.

5. Begin by planting the box trees, keeping them to the same depth as they were in their original pots. Next plant out the cyclamen along the centre of the box and, finally, position the ivies along the front. Try to keep the planting evenly spaced so that the box looks symmetrical.

6. Firm down the compost and level it to about 2.5cm (1in) below the rim.

7. Alternatively, leave all the plants in their pots and simply arrange these in the window box. This prevents their roots being disturbed and makes it easier to use them again.

8. Whichever method is used, water when planting is complete.

MAINTENANCE

Water in dry spells but do not over-water. Replace the cyclamen as the flowers fade or if unexpected frosts kill them.

Pansies Galore

THIS IS ONE of the simplest of window boxes to create, but it is none the worse for that. Plant six pansies in a basic trough, and you will have a display that will last through the winter months and well into spring. Alternatively, if you plant it in spring, you will have flowers throughout summer and well into autumn. There are many possible variations on the theme of just two different varieties, and you can ring the changes according to your own preferences and what is available.

INGREDIENTS

3 blotched pansies (*Viola* 'Universal Plus Ivory/Rose Blotch') **(A)**
3 blue pansies (*Viola* 'Universal Plus True Blue') **(B)**

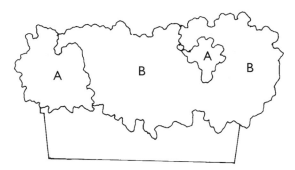

CONTAINER

White plastic trough
45cm (18in) long; 12.5cm (5in) wide; 12.5cm (5in) deep

MATERIALS

Pieces of old pottery or broken tiles
2.5cm (1in) layer of gravel or small stones
General potting compost to fill container

POSITION

In winter this arrangement needs a sunny window-sill, but in summer it should be in partial shade because pansies do not like to be too hot.

PLANTING

1. For winter use, plant this box in autumn; for summer use, plant in spring.

2. Places pieces of broken pottery over the drainage holes so that the compost and gravel will not be washed out but excess water can drain away.

3. Cover the bottom of the box with a 2.5cm (1in) layer of gravel to improve the drainage.

4. Fill the window box with a general potting compost.

5. Mark a regular pattern for the pansies, then start planting at one end. Even with only six pansies of two varieties several different designs can be created. For example, four blue pansies could be planted in an arc, two at the ends and two at the back, while two blotched ones could be planted in the centre front.

6. Gently firm the compost around the plants and level the surface just below the top of the window box.

7. Water.

MAINTENANCE

Pansies do not like to dry out completely so make sure that the soil is always moist. Winter displays will not want as much water as summer ones. Feed monthly in winter, weekly in summer. Remove dead flowerheads as they appear. If the plants grow straggly, cut them back and they will re-shoot.

Two into One

THESE WINDOW BOXES are too beautiful to be hidden behind a profusion of trailing foliage. Here, the trailing ivy only partially obscures the boxes, heightening the viewer's interest in them. The focus is the bright red florist's cyclamen. These are frost tender and can be used only in the warmer town centres or in milder areas. The boxes are identical and can be used in multiples for windows of different sizes on the same building.

INGREDIENTS

(Each box)
1 young conifer (*Chamaecyparis*) **(A)**
1 bright red florist's cyclamen (*Cyclamen*) **(B)**
1 red-budded skimmia (*Skimmia japonica* 'Rubella') **(C)**
1 variegated ivy (*Hedera helix* 'Eva') **(D)**
1 variegated hebe (*Hebe × franciscana* 'Variegata') **(E)**

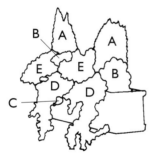

CONTAINER

2 terracotta window boxes
Each box 30cm long; 20cm (8in) wide; 25cm (10in) deep

MATERIALS

Pieces of old pots or broken tiles
2.5cm (1in) layer of gravel or small stones
Lime-free (ericaceous) compost to fill container

POSITION

This must be in a warm position, or the cyclamen can be killed. A place that receives the winter sun would be best.

PLANTING

1. Plant up the box in autumn but wait until the cyclamen is in flower before adding it to the arrangement.

2. Cover the drainage holes so that excess water can easily drain away but the gravel and potting compost are not washed out.

3. Add a 2.5cm (1in) layer of gravel or small stones to the bottom of the box to improve drainage.

4. Fill the boxes with potting compost. Use a lime-free compost mixture because the skimmia is happier in acidic conditions.

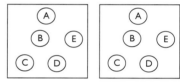

5. Plant the conifer well towards the back, leaving plenty of room for the other plants. Then plant the skimmia and the hebe. Position the ivy at the front so that it can trail over the edge. Do not plant the cyclamen too deep – the top of the corm should be level with the surface.

6. Gently firm down the compost around the plants and level the surface so that it is about 2.5cm (1in) below the rim.

7. Water.

MAINTENANCE

Because this is a winter display, there is no need to water unless the weather is exceptionally dry or the box is sheltered from the rain. Do not make it too wet. Feed once a month. Replace the cyclamen when it finishes flowering.

Winter Joy

*T*HIS IS A *well-balanced display that will provide interest throughout the whole of winter and into spring. The dark red buds of the skimmias are beautifully complemented by their dark foliage and by that of the heucheras and the gaultherias. The red berries of the gaultherias also work in well. The white laurustinus buds and flowers make a fine contrast. The cascade of ivy neatly finishes off the picture. This is an easy, trouble-free display that is well worth making.*

INGREDIENTS

1 laurustinus (*Viburnum tinus*) **(A)**
2 red-budded skimmias (*Skimmia japonica* 'Rubella') **(B)**
2 gaultherias (*Gaultheria procumbens*) **(C)**
2 purple-leaved heucheras (*Heuchera micrantha* 'Palace Purple')
(D)
4 variegated ivies (*Hedera helix* 'Glacier') **(E)**

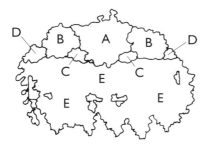

CONTAINER

Wooden window box, painted white
90cm (36in) long; 15cm (6in) wide; 15cm (6in) deep

MATERIALS

Pieces of old pottery or broken tiles
2.5cm (1in) layer of gravel or small stones
Lime-free (ericaceous) compost to fill container

POSITION

This window box can be positioned anywhere as long
as it is not too dark.

PLANTING

1. This box can be planted at any time but autumn is best.

2. Cover the drainage holes so that the compost and gravel are kept within the box while excess water can drain away freely.

3. Cover the bottom 2.5cm (1in) of the window box with gravel or small stones.

4. Fill the container with a lime-free potting compost. It must be lime-free or the skimmias will not thrive.

5. Plant the laurustinus towards the back in the centre of the box. Place a skimmia on either side, leaving just enough space to tuck the gaultherias between them. At the far ends on the box plant the heucheras. Finally, plant the ivies along the front of the box so that they can trail over the edge.

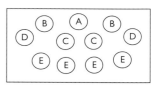

6. Firm down the soil between the plants and level the surface so that it is about 2.5cm (1in) below the top of the box.

7. Water.

MAINTENANCE

Little maintenance is required. Water sparingly in winter and only when the compost begins to dry out. Feed once every month, more frequently if there is a lot of rain. Remove any dead leaves or flowerheads as they appear.

Winter Warmth

*W*ARM COLOURS ARE *ideal for winter compositions. They help to relieve the chilly weather and cheer us up during the bleakest months. This imaginative design not only includes rich reds but also uses bronze-foliaged ivy as well. Even the touch of frost that lingers on it is not enough to dim its warmth. The box is rather deep given the height of the display, but the trailing ivies help to disguise this. The box illustrated is dark blue – white or black would be equally attractive.*

INGREDIENTS

1 red-budded skimmia (*Skimmia japonica* 'Rubella') **(A)**
2 cut-leaf ornamental kales (*Brassica oleracea*) **(B)**
6 winter-flowering heathers (*Erica carnea* 'Vivellii') **(C)**
2 variegated ivies (*Hedera helix* 'Glacier') **(D)**
1 bronze variegated ivy (*Hedera helix* 'Multicolor') **(E)**

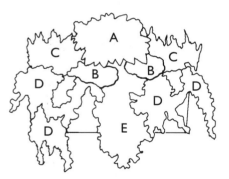

CONTAINER

Wooden window box, painted blue
50cm (20in) long; 15cm (6in) wide; 20cm (8in) deep

MATERIALS

Pieces of old pottery or broken roof tiles
2.5cm (1in) layer of gravel or small stones
Lime-free (ericaceous) compost to fill container

POSITION

Any site will do for this container, although a sunny one would be best.

PLANTING

1. This window box can be assembled at any time during autumn or early winter.

2. Cover the drainage holes with pieces of old pottery or irregularly shaped stones so that excess water can drain away, but the gravel and compost cannot be washed out.

3. Fill the bottom of the box with a 2.5cm (1in) layer of gravel or small stones to improve the drainage.

4. Use a lime-free compost because the heathers will not tolerate a soil with lime in it.

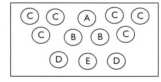

5. Plant the skimmia in the centre back of the box. The six heathers can be planted, three on either side, with ornamental kales tucked under the skimmia. If space is tight and the plants are large, one kale may be sufficient. The two plain variegated ivies should be positioned next, planted towards the corners, so that the trailing stems can be trained over the three visible sides. Finally, fill in the centre space with the multicoloured ivy.

6. Gently press down the compost and level the surface so that it is about 2.5cm (1in) below the rim of the box.

7. Water.

MAINTENANCE

Water only when necessary. Feed monthly. Remove any leaves of the kale that die back.

Pinnacle of Elegance

*A*S WELL AS *simplicity, elegance is a worthy attribute to strive for when designing window boxes. This one possesses that quality. The graceful way the shapes in the background build up to the pinnacle while the flowering plants float on a sea of ivy is a pleasurable sight. This is a box for winter and spring, when the primulas are beginning to burst forth. Cyclamen, alas, are tender and need to be replaced if they get frosted during a cold spell.*

INGREDIENTS

1 columnar juniper (*Juniper communis* 'Compressa') **(A)**
4 box topiaries (*Buxus sempervirens*) **(B)**
2 red florist's cyclamen (*Cyclamen*) **(C)**
2 gaultherias (*Gaultheria procumbens*) **(D)**
5 white primrose hybrids (*Primula*) **(E)**
6 variegated ivies (*Hedera helix* 'Glacier') **(F)**
2 white winter-flowering heathers (*Erica carnea* 'Springwood White') **(G)**

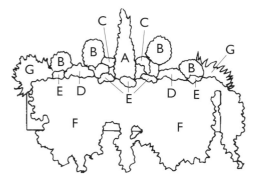

CONTAINER

Wooden window box, painted white
90cm (36in) long; 15cm (6in) wide; 15cm (6in) deep

MATERIALS

Pieces of old pottery or broken tiles
2.5cm (1in) layer of gravel or small stones
Lime-free (ericaceous) compost to fill container

POSITION

A frost-free site is required unless the plants can be protected. Both full sun and partial shade are suitable.

PLANTING

1. Make up the box when the cyclamen or the primulas are in flower.

2. Cover the drainage holes with a piece of pottery so that excess water can drain away but the compost is held back.

3. Add a layer of about 2.5cm (1in) gravel or small stones to the bottom of the box to improve the drainage.

4. Fill the box with a lime-free compost because heathers prefer acidic conditions.

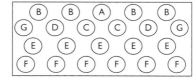

5. The tall juniper should be planted first. Next position the topiaried box trees, keeping them well to the back of the box. Plant the two cyclamen on either side of the juniper and the gaultherias between the box trees. The next row consists of the five primroses, with the heathers tucked in at the ends. The ivies go along the front of the box.

6. Firm down the compost and level it so that the surface is about 2.5cm (1in) below the top of the box. Water.

MAINTENANCE

Water when required and feed every two weeks.

Nodding Acquaintance

LIKE MANY OLD-FASHIONED flowers, pansies have a quality about them that is instantly reminiscent of childhood. They make ideal plants for window boxes because they are brought up to eye-level, where they can be appreciated to the full. They work well with other plants, or they can be planted on their own as here. These two single-coloured varieties work very well together.

INGREDIENTS

2 golden pansies (*Viola* 'Forerunner Orange') **(A)**
2 purple pansies (*Viola* 'Oxford Blue') **(B)**

9 tulip bulbs (*Tulipa*)
9 snowdrops (*Galanthus nivalis*)

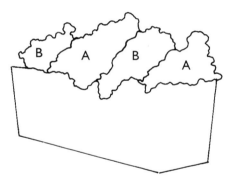

CONTAINER

Wooden window box, painted black
45cm (18in) long; 15cm (6in) wide; 20cm (8in) deep

MATERIALS

Pieces of broken pottery or old tiles
2.5cm (1in) layer of gravel or small stones
General potting compost to fill container

POSITION

Pansies do not like to get too hot, so for a summer display
do not place it where it will be in the midday sun.

PLANTING

1. For a winter scheme, plant in autumn or when the plants are ready. For a summer display, plant in spring.

2. Cover the drainage holes with pieces of broken pottery so that excess water can drain away but compost and gravel are retained in the box.

3. Fill the bottom of the box with about 2.5cm (1in) of gravel or small stones to improve the drainage.

4. Fill the rest of the window box with a general potting compost.

5. This box is easy to plant. Simply space out the four plants in a straight line, alternating the colours. A winter and spring display can be further enlivened by planting snowdrops and tulips among the pansies. Half fill the box with compost and plant the tulip bulbs along the back. Continue to fill the box until it is three-quarters full and then plant the snowdrops in what will be the gaps between the pansies. Fill the box and plant the pansies.

6. Firm down the compost between the plants and level the surface, which should be about 2.5cm (1in) below the top of the box.

7. Water.

MAINTENANCE

Water sparingly in winter, but more frequently in summer. Feed weekly in summer. Cut back the pansies if they become too straggly.

Laurel and Heather

*T*HIS IS AN *extremely simple window box and yet the result is very effective. The contrast between the heathers and the spotted laurel is startling and eye-catching. One of the great advantages of using heathers in winter window boxes is that even when they have finished flowering the dead flowers still look attractive. Here, the brown remains of the flowers work as well, if not better, with the green and gold laurel as the rose-pink blooms did.*

INGREDIENTS

1 spotted laurel (*Aucuba japonica* 'Gold Dust') **(A)**
2 rose-pink heathers (*Erica carnea* 'Vivellii') **(B)**

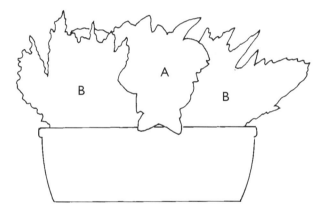

CONTAINER

Terracotta window box
35cm (14in) long; 15cm (6in) wide; 15cm (6in) deep

MATERIALS

Pieces of broken pottery or tiles
2.5cm (1in) layer of gravel or small stones
Lime-free (ericaceous) compost to fill container

POSITION

Either sun or partial shade will be suitable for this window box.

PLANTING

1. Plant this box any time between autumn and late winter, but avoid times when the weather is particularly cold.

2. Cover the drainage holes in the bottom of the box with pieces of broken pottery so that water can freely drain away but the compost and gravel are prevented from falling out.

3. The bottom of the box should be covered with a layer of about 2.5cm (1in) of gravel or small stones to improve the drainage.

4. Fill the box with lime-free compost because heathers dislike limy conditions.

5. Plant the spotted laurel in the centre of the box, with the heathers on either side. Depending on the size of your box and the size of the heathers you may need a few more plants to fill the space.

6. Gently firm down the compost around the plants and level the surface so that it is about 2.5cm (1in) below the edge of the window box.

7. Water.

MAINTENANCE

Water sparingly in winter and only when the compost begins to dry out. If you want to use only flowering plants and not those with the remains of the dried-up blooms, replant with fresh heathers as soon as the existing ones begin to fade. For a summer show, replace the winter-flowering heathers with summer-flowering types.

All-year Display

*T*HIS IS A *display that can be used all-year round. In many respects it might be considered rather dull in that it is all green — and a solid mass of green at that — but, in fact, many people will find the simple shapes and colour a relief from some of the more flamboyant window boxes. It can be used as a foil for things to come. Here, for example, the tips of hyacinths are beginning to show. Later, pots of tulips can be slipped in followed by summer plants of your choice.*

INGREDIENTS

4 shaped box (*Buxus sempervirens*) (A)
8 trailing ivies (*Hedera helix*) (B)

5 pots of bulbs, cyclamen or summer plants of your choice

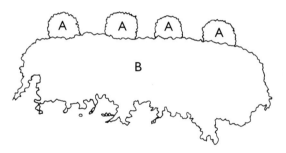

CONTAINER

2 wooden containers
Overall size 180cm (6ft) long; 20cm (8in) wide;
20cm (8in) deep

MATERIALS

Pieces of broken pottery or tiles
2.5cm (1in) layer of gravel or small stones
General potting compost to fill container

POSITION

This display can be positioned in any position, including shade. If summer plants are used then a sunnier position may be necessary.

PLANTING

1. This arrangement can be planted at any time during the year.

2. Cover the draining holes in the bottom of the boxes with pieces of pottery so that excess water can drain away, while the compost and gravel are not washed away.

3. Add a layer of about 2.5cm (1in) of gravel or small stones to keep the compost well drained.

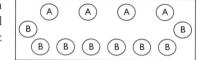

4. Fill the box with a general potting compost.

5. Plant the box at regular intervals along the back half of the box. In front of these plant the ivies so that they trail down over the front edge.

6. Firm down the compost between the plants so that the final level is about 2.5cm (1in) below the top of the box.

7. Water.

8. Further plants can be added when required. These can be planted into the compost in the normal way but are probably best left in the pots, especially if they are already in flower. The pots are bedded directly into the compost.

MAINTENANCE

Water when the soil begins to dry out. More frequent watering is required in summer than in winter. Similarly, feed monthly in winter but every 10 days in the summer. Clip over the box shrubs to keep them neat.

Choosing a window box

THERE IS A SURPRISINGLY large choice of window boxes available. They can be found not only in garden centres and nurseries but also in those fascinating places that are half-way between an open-air shop and a factory and that produce garden statuary and ornaments. You can, of course, also make window boxes yourself, although if you do, you are going to be restricted largely to wooden ones.

There are three main types of window box. First, there are the decorative ones, which are worth looking at for their own sakes. Terracotta containers are a good example of this kind. Second, there are utilitarian boxes. These are boxes that are intended simply to hold plants, and they need not be anything special because they are likely to be covered up most of the time by trailing plants. The third category is really nothing more elaborate than a container, because the box consists of a plastic trough in which a window display is prepared in advance and then slipped inside a more decorative box when the time comes to put it in place.

The decorative boxes are, obviously, more expensive, but if they are treated carefully they will last a lifetime. They will also allow you to produce the widest range of displays, because you will not be worried about creating something that does not cover at least part of the box with its flowing lines. Plain window boxes are fine for most purposes, but they can sometimes look a bit boring and angular if all the plants rise above them, rather than disguising their shape. The choice of colour may help to disguise it or soften the lines.

SHAPE

It might seem that there is not much to think about when it comes to the shape of the box, but there are, in fact, several aspects that can affect your choice. The conventional box is rectangular, but there is no need for this to be so. The simplest variation is to have a box with rounded ends. These shapes are usually made from terracotta, but if you would prefer something more unconventional, you could use an old galvanized bath, for example, provided that you have a sill or brackets wide enough to hold it securely in position.

Another possibility is to use round pots. Instead of a single long box, a row of ordinary terracotta flowerpots can be extremely effective. Similarly, several larger tubs may be used.

The simple plastic window box works perfectly in this setting – the white colour goes well with the lilac and pink flowers.

The main problem with individual pots and containers is security. It is not too difficult to secure a box to the sill, but smaller containers are more difficult to fasten in place and can easily be knocked or blown off.

Rows of pots are particularly suitable if you want to grow a single type of plant. Anyone who has seen window-sills filled with the pots of scarlet geraniums that are so popular in continental Europe, will know what a glorious sight they can be. These pots seem somehow to be part of the plant and are essential to the picture created.

Individual pots can, of course, be placed within a conventional window box, and in some cases this can be an advantage – for example, you may have a plant whose roots you did not want to disturb or a short-lived plant that you want to be able to remove easily from the display and replace with another.

Half-pots can be used to fix on the wall below small windows. For larger windows and in place of conventional window boxes, some gardeners use real or mock hay-racks. These are usually nothing more than metal frameworks, and to make them usable as window boxes you will need to provide an inner lining to hold the compost and plants as you would with a hanging basket.

SIZE

The size of the box is important. Ideally, the box should fit the available space – it should be the same length as the window and, when it is placed on the sill, it should be the same width. In practice, this is not always possible because windows are frequently odd sizes and you cannot buy boxes that will fit exactly. If you are making the boxes yourself, of course, this should not be a problem. If the box is only a bit shorter than the window, selecting plants that will trail over the ends of the container and hide the gaps will make the box seem longer.

If you are using window boxes on several floors, it is possible that the size of the window openings will vary at each level and each of the boxes will need to be a different size. For wide window openings it is possible to use two or more boxes, placed end to end. Remember that the larger the box

This wooden box is painted white which suits the pale colour scheme of the plants.

the heavier it will be if you have to move it, and two shorter ones will often be easier to cope with than one long one. Size and weight must also be considered in terms of how much the window-sill or brackets can support. Do not overload a weak or doubtful structure.

COLOUR

The colour of a window box is important. Terracotta boxes have a natural earthy colour that goes well with most forms of planting. It has a warm, sympathetic look that, even when it is stained white and green with salts and algae and has the patina of age, is still the perfect foil for all kinds of plants.

Wooden, concrete and plastic boxes do not have that advantage, but these materials can always be painted. White and black are the two favourite colours. White goes well with white-painted walls and with white window-frames, and it is often a sympathetic colour for many plants. Sometimes,

A row of individual pots on a window-sill creates a display that has impact when viewed from either side of the window.

however, white can be too bright, and it will show up, for example, through trailing plants when it might be best if the box is not seen. Another disadvantage is that it does not weather well and may need frequent repainting, usually more often than the house, because of the moisture in the box.

Black boxes generally look well against brick and stone walls and a house's black paintwork. Black has the additional advantage that it seems to disappear when trailing plants hang over it, creating the illusion that the plants are suspended in space or clinging to the wall. Dark green can have the same effect.

Window boxes are frequently painted the same colour as the house woodwork. A red front door means red window boxes, but this can begin to look a bit garish and out of character if the colour is overdone. However if the house has

shutters around the windows it is a good idea to treat the window boxes in the same way as the shutters.

Boxes can, of course, be painted whatever colour you like, and if you have the time and resources, you can change the colour to suit the display you are creating. They can match the colours of the dominant flower or be painted to provide a contrast to it.

If you plan to use trailing plants and therefore feel that the colour of the box is irrelevant, remember that when the plants are young or just planted they may not cover the entire box and so its colour will show.

Decoration on window boxes is a matter of choice. Boxes made of terracotta, moulded concrete and reconstituted stone often have motifs or geometric patterns on them, which can be very attractive. Moulding can also be an appealing feature on wooden boxes, but additional decorations such as coloured tiles can detract from the display. Occasionally, however, they can be fun. Bits of broken pottery and mirror applied to boxes for a building in hot sun, or sea shells on boxes decorating seaside houses will often work perfectly. Such additions should be used with caution, however, for in the wrong place or overdone they will merely look rather vulgar.

MATERIALS

The material from which the window box is made is a very important consideration. Not only does it affect the cost and the appearance but also the weight that must be supported and the ease with which it can be moved.

TERRACOTTA

For many window box gardeners, terracotta will always be considered the preferred material. The appearance is sympathetic to a wide range of plantings, they are attractive in their own right, and they are very well suited for use with displays when the container is in full view and not covered with trailing plants. Almost any colour of flower or foliage seems to go well the warm reddish colour of the clay. In addition to being ideal for full-scale window boxes, terracotta is also a

perfect material for smaller containers, including ordinary flowerpots of various sizes.

There are disadvantages to terracotta. In the first place, window boxes made from it are likely to be very expensive, although with care they will last a lifetime and will long outlast those made from other materials. From a practical point of view, they are heavy. This means that they are best put in position and planted in situ, rather than the display being prepared in the comfort of a greenhouse or conservatory or even on the ground. It also means that they will have to have a solid support. A strong window-sill or, better still, a small balcony will be needed. It is possible to hold them on brackets, but this is not as suitable a means of support as for, say, wooden boxes, and there are rarely suitable fixing points. It is not just the weight of the box that must be considered – you must also think about the combined weight of the compost and water. The terracotta itself will absorb a large

A beautiful display, enhanced by a decorative container. The window box is made of wood and has small wall tiles stuck to it.

amount of water, thus adding to the weight. Despite the difficulties associated with holding them securely in place, the total weight of a planted terracotta container usually means that it will not blow off a window-sill.

Another disadvantage of terracotta is that poorer quality containers of this material can shatter in hard frosts. Window recesses and walls normally provide some protection, and window boxes are not so prone to freezing as containers that are standing out in the open. However, if you live in an area that is prone to sharp frosts, this is something you may need to take into consideration.

Apart from its appearance, terracotta has other advantages as a material for containers in which plants are grown. The evaporation of moisture from its surface means that it remains cool in the summer, yet its nature is such that it is relatively

A small window box safely held by decorative railings round the sill. The black window box blends with the ironwork.

warm in winter, thus protecting the roots of plants from extremes of temperature. The loss of water through its porous sides also means that it is very difficult to over-water a terracotta window box, which is an important consideration because nearly all plants detest being waterlogged.

WOOD

The other traditional material is wood, which has many advantages. It is a relatively inexpensive material, and it is easily worked. Wooden window boxes can be purchased ready-made or you can make them yourself. If you are handy or know someone who is, you use scraps of timber, thus reducing the cost considerably. Ready-made boxes will be the standard sizes, but if you make them yourself or have them made, they can be tailored to suit your own requirements. Although this is an important consideration if you want to fit them to your window-sills, it is even more crucial if the sills

are protected by iron railings and the box has to fit inside these.

Unless they are made of hardwood, wooden window boxes are liable to rot, and they must, therefore, be treated with a preservative. Make sure that you use a preparation that does not harm plants – creosote, for example, should be avoided. The alternative, and it is usually the preferred option, is to paint them.

PLASTIC

Many gardeners think that plastic has a reputation for being a rather nasty material, and so it can be when it is used badly or inappropriately. When it comes to window boxes, however, it has the advantage of being cheap and light. Window boxes made of plastic can easily be prepared on the ground and then moved – which usually involves lifting – into place. However, even these, when full of moist compost, weigh a great deal, and unless you are strong and fit, it is generally better to fill and plant them in situ.

One of the disadvantages of plastic is that even if it has been manufactured to look like something else, it always seems to look like what it really is – plastic. In addition, plastic boxes are not as easily painted as other materials and you are, therefore, usually stuck with the original colour. Visually, plastic is not a very sympathetic material when it is combined with plants, but if the window box is going to be planted with trailing plants that will spill leaves and tendrils over the sides of the box, this will not be important.

Because of their lightness and lack of bulk, plastic window boxes are ideal for slipping inside other containers. This is a particularly useful characteristic for 'quick change' displays. A new display can be prepared in advance of the time it should go out, so that the plants are all fully developed or are in full flower. When the old display is ready to be discarded, it is a relatively simple procedure to remove one inner box and replace it with another. Wooden and terracotta boxes make ideal outer cases.

It is possible to buy plastic window boxes that have been specially designed to be self-watering. These are particularly useful for windows that are not easy or convenient to reach for regular daily watering.

OTHER MATERIALS

Usually lumped together with plastic in most people's minds is fibreglass. This is increasingly being used for garden containers, including window boxes. Some are relatively plain and not much better than ordinary plastic, but others are reproductions of terracotta and lead containers that are so faithful to the original that it is impossible to see that they are not what they appear without touching them. The textures and colours are reproduced with great fidelity, as are all the details, down to the marks and imperfections of the original. Unfortunately, these are very expensive –often nearly as costly as the object they are made to resemble.

Lead used to be used for all manner of garden containers and decorative articles, but for all practical purposes it is not a consideration for today's gardeners, delightful though these pieces are.

Window boxes made from cement, concrete or reconstituted stone are also available, but on the whole they are rather heavy and have no real advantage over other materials. At one time they were more readily obtainable than terracotta, but this is no longer true as terracotta has been used to make a wide variety of shapes and styles. When it comes to a permanent planting, the weight of concrete and reconstituted stone has the advantage that the boxes are unlikely to be blown off the sill and will not require fixing. Against this, however, must be placed the difficulty of moving a full container of these materials.

There are other kinds of other boxes and containers that can be adapted for use as window boxes, but do remember that whatever you choose should be a little more than just a container for plants. It will be seen and should, therefore, have some qualities of its own to add to the whole picture. If you choose a container other than one that has been specifically made as a window box, you are likely to find that it has no drainage holes. These are essential and you will have to drill holes in the base to compensate for their absence.

Style and content

STYLE AND DESIGN are two aspects of gardening that sometimes frighten people who feel that they have no artistic
ability or that they ought to have a special knowledge of
design techniques and colour theory before they can even
begin to create their own window boxes. This is, of course,
not true. Anybody can put together a display of plants that
will give pleasure to themselves and others.

Most people feel comfortable in the clothes they wear and
the decoration of the houses in which they live. Almost

A row of boxes planted to the same design complements the formal
façade of this building.

instinctively, they know what colours suit them and how to
combine certain items of clothing to get the effect they want.
Not everyone would necessarily agree with the result – it
would be a dull world if they did – but the wearer is usually
happy. Similarly, most people manage to decorate their houses
to their own satisfaction. There may be a few dramas and
difficulties on the way, but on the whole, most people will say
that they like what they achieve.

It is the same with designing a window box. The first prin-
ciple is to create something that you like rather than something that would grace a stately home. An appropriate choice
of clothing is something we learn as we grow up, and most of
us are probably not even conscious that we are learning – it is
simply a skill we seem to acquire. In gardening the same
happens: the more you make, the better you become and the
less you worry about it.

The idea behind this book is that you should start by
copying in detail some of the designs so that you get a feel for
creating a display. Then, as you gain confidence, you can start
to alter elements of the designs to make them more of your
own choice, and eventually you will want to design boxes on
your own. It is worth remembering that most window boxes
are created by people who would claim to have no artistic
ability, who have never read a book on design and who have
never attended a course on it. With a book to guide your first
steps, you are off to a flying start.

SELECTING PLANTS

Before looking at the actual design, it is worth thinking about
the plants with which you can work. There is really no bar to

the plants you can use, with the possible exception of water plants, but even these could be incorporated with a little ingenuity and might make some exciting arrangements.

Some plants are conventionally thought of as container plants. These are mainly annuals, although a few common perennials, shrubs and climbers are usually included as well. Petunias, geraniums (*Pelargonium*), busy lizzies, lobelias, pansies, heathers, fuchsias and ivies provide plenty of flower and foliage colour and a great variety in shape. Common as these are, there is absolutely nothing wrong with them, and you could spend a lifetime producing interesting and varied boxes with them. Nearly all are available in a wide range of varieties, which means that you can create either bright, colourful displays or softer, more subtle ones.

The true window box addict, however, is not content with such a restricted palette. There are thousands of different plants, and most of them can be used in window boxes with varying degrees of success. If you always buy your bedding plants from your local garden centre or nursery, you may find yourself somewhat limited for choice, but the moment you pick up a seed catalogue (usually free from the major seed merchants) you will see that the world of annuals and bedding stretches far beyond these plants. For a start, you will probably be amazed at the wide variety of common plants that you buy – yellow petunias and double lobelias, for example. Then there are the less common plants – the delightful starry isotoma (also called laurentia), lovely silenes, asarinas, nemophilas and so on – and there is no reason you should not elevate some of the border annuals to the window box – marigolds, dwarf cornflowers, tobacco plants, mimulus and love-lies-bleeding, to name just a few.

The garden can also be a source of inspiration if you look at the large number of perennial plants that are suitable. How about including bleeding heart in your late spring displays? The golden flowers of the smaller leopard's banes would brighten a spring box. Diascias would certainly be a good choice for the summer. Foliage plants such as hostas, ferns and the silver artemisias could also be very useful.

As well as perennials why not try a few shrubs? Young conifers, before they grow too large for containers, can be used to create wonderful backgrounds and add structure to a display. If you have the patience, you can train box bushes into various shapes, which can be used time and again. These can be simple geometric shapes or something more ambitious. Shrubs can be used without taking them out of their pots so that they can be used again in subsequent displays. One of the most valuable shrubs that has become very popular in recent years for winter window boxes is the red-budded skimmia, *Skimmia japonica* 'Rubella'.

Climbing plants are not much used in window boxes, but their potential is enormous – they can go up or down. Planted in the corners of a window box, they can be allowed to climb up wires or a trellis beside the window to frame it, or they can be allowed to tumble over the edge of the box and cascade down. Ivies are an obvious choice, but clematis, morning glories, black-eyed Susan and many others can be used. It important if you try this that the boxes are not in a windy position, or the results might be disappointing.

Another rich vein to explore would be indoor plants. Although most of these are too tender to survive outside in winter, many will be more than happy to grow in the open in the summer. Spider plants, coleus, tradescantias and even aspidistras can make a valuable contribution to a window box arrangement.

There is little point in growing vegetables in a window box because it would be impossible to grow enough to harvest more than a mouthful. There are, however, one or two decorative vegetables, such as ornamental cabbages and kale, that may be worth considering. Herbs can be grown to advantage, for many have attractive foliage as well as being useful and popular for cutting for the kitchen. Parsley makes a good foliage plant, while chives have pretty purple flowers, and both are among the most used herbs in cooking.

DESIGN CONSIDERATIONS

Having thought about the plants you want to use, you should now think about what you want to do with them. It is, of course, possible simply to push them into the window box without much thought as to any arrangement – much as many people do with cut flowers. This rather hit-and-miss method may work, but it is more satisfactory to attempt to make a more positive display.

COLOUR

First, let us consider colour. Certain colours are regarded as being 'hot'. Bright reds, oranges and the orange shades of yellow – gold for example – fall into the group. Hot colours tend to be exciting. They are party colours, which add gaiety and fun to a scene. As with all excitement, too much can become tiring, even boring, so the important thing is to know when to stop. Window boxes are usually small and discrete, so it is possible to get away with wholesale use of hot colours, but beware of transforming the whole façade of your house because it may be overwhelming.

'Cool' colours, on the other hand – soft blues, mauves, pinks and whites, for example – are usually soft and gentle to the eye. They have the opposite effect of hot colours and tend to calm things down, creating an air of peace and tranquillity. If you want to create a romantic atmosphere, the softer, dreamy colours are the ones to use. Mixing a few pink blooms into a box of reds will cool the scheme down, taking the edge off the intensity. It will also add more interest to the scheme.

Colours vary in their relationship with each other. Some colours blend together well and appear to be sympathetic towards each other. For example, blues and purples blend well together as do purples and reds. Yellows and greens also associate pleasantly, as do yellows and oranges, although the effects that will result from mixing, say, yellow and orange, will be different from the effects you will get from mixing yellow and green.

Other colours tend to contrast with each other. These are known as complementary colours – yellow and blue, for instance, or red and green. In both cases, the two colours are a stark contrast to one another, giving a fresh, clear-cut image.

When you start to mix colours in a window box you have to do it with care to get the effect you want. Too many colours mixed together will make the overall effect look bitty or spotty. This is because there is nowhere for the eye to come to rest. It wanders over the display, vainly looking for something on which to stop. However, if you have a few muted colours and one bright one, the eye will go straight to it because the single bright colour acts as a focal point. In a planting scheme, therefore, you would want to put such a plant towards the middle or the top. It would be a bizarre scheme that wanted to draw the eye to, say, the lower left-hand corner.

When you are considering colour you are not just thinking of flower colour – foliage plays an important part, too. There are hundreds of shades of green, and so it is always possible to make the most of flower and foliage colour. Bright red, for example, looks fresher and brighter against dark green than it does against a yellow-green, and it has quite a different appearance against bronze or purple. Remember that the texture of leaves can also influence colour. The pink blooms of an ivy-leaved geranium, seen against its shiny leaves, will have a different effect from the same pink of a zonal geranium, which has matt green leaves. Shiny foliage reflects the light and looks especially good in shady areas.

Foliage colour is not restricted to green. It may be yellow, gold, silver, grey, blue, purple, red and many shades between. Then there are multi-coloured leaves – variegated foliage – to consider. Here the range includes green and gold, green and silver as well as triple colours such as green, cream and purple.

These, then, are just some of the aspects of colour that you should bear in mind when you start to construct a window box. Above all, try to bring sympathetic colours together and avoid creating spotty effects. Grade colours from one to another except where you want to make an impact, and then do it with contrasting colours. Avoid having too many contrasting colours in one scheme. Occasionally, there is no harm in wishing to make a statement and doing everything you shouldn't, but do it with conviction and don't do it too often, or it will become boring.

Before you commit yourself to a particular scheme, place all the plants together on the ground, still in their pots, just as you think you might plant them. Juggle them around, perhaps taking some out and adding others until you are reasonably satisfied. Whole books have been written about flower and foliage colour and how they relate to one another, but the best way of finding out about it is to enjoy yourself and experiment. If your experiments do not work, it is easy enough to take a display apart, and there is always next year to try again.

SHAPE AND PROPORTION

Individual plants vary greatly in their shape. Some are round – they squat down and look comfortable. Other plants are spiky and spring up in a fountain of excitement. Using plants that all the same shape can be safe but is just as likely to be boring. A mixture of forms is usually more interesting.

The overall shape of the box is also important. In some arrangements the display is upright and angular; in others, trailing and flopping plants soften the edges and make them look more romantic. Spring displays frequently include bulbs, most of which are upright, giving the impression that they are springing straight from the earth to celebrate a new year. It is, after all, the time of year when sap rises in both plants and gardeners. Later, everything, including the gardener, begins to sag under the progress of summer, and softer, tumbling designs seem more appropriate.

Try to build up the shape towards the centre of the box or just to one side of centre. It looks odd if the highest part of the display is right to one side or the other. It may seem obvious, but if one group of plants is taller than another, plant these towards the back and the shorter ones to the front. It could be argued that window boxes are looked at from the inside as well as from the outside of the house, but if you put shorter plants against the window, the taller ones will block their light and they will soon become leggy and etiolated. If you want to see the box from both sides, choose plants that are all the same height.

Symmetrical shapes are the most appropriate for formal schemes, but for a more informal approach, try moving the dominant plants so that they are off-centre and create a blurring effect around the edges by using trailing plants.

Some of the most successful window box arrangements are the simplest – displays that are limited to one, two or perhaps three types of plant. When more plants types are

A riot of colour and shapes creates a cottage garden in miniature that looks well against this brick wall.

introduced, the arrangement begins to look more complicated and it will have lost its appealing simplicity. A planting of just one variety, such as a bed of pansies or a block of geraniums, is one of the easiest displays you can devise.

Above all, remember that you are creating the window box for yourself. You should, therefore, do what makes you feel comfortable and create something that you personally enjoy. Not everybody will agree with you, but that is perhaps their loss.

Site

THE POSITIONING OF window boxes may seem to be nothing more than putting a box on a window-sill. Needless to say, there is a little more to it than that. What, for example, if your windows open outwards?

Certainly, the best position is on the window-sill if there is one. Frequently, however, the sill is not wide enough to take the whole width of the box. Whatever you do, do not leave the box so that part of it overhangs the edge of the sill. This is extremely dangerous, for a sudden gust of wind or a cat jumping on it can easily dislodge it. A falling box will not only break and destroy its contents, but it could well fall on somebody and seriously injure, or even kill them. Even really heavy containers, such as those made of terracotta, which are unlikely to be dislodged, will, if they do for some reason fall off, cause a great deal of damage. One way of coping with the problem is to fix brackets below the box to give it some extra stability. Alternatively, a wider ledge, again supported by brackets, can be created.

Even when your window-sill is wide enough to accommodate the full width of a box, you can still have problems. Sills are designed to shed any rain that falls on the window, and so they usually slope away from the frame. Any box that is placed directly on a sloping sill will eventually slide off, and remember, too, that a window box at an angle will look rather odd. These problems can be corrected by inserting tapered wedges under the box so that it is levelled. Wedges also have the advantage that they raise the box slightly from the sill, so any excess water can drain away easily through the drainage holes.

It is essential that you prevent the box from falling off the sill. Wind is probably the worst enemy because it can easily cause a seemingly stable box to fall off a window-sill in a sudden gust. Hooks fastened into the wall or window-frame are the best way of coping with the problem of wind. These engage in eyes located on the ends of the box. The windowbox can be wired or even nailed to the wall or frame, but they are then not easy to remove, and it does not do the window-frame much good to have nails or screws repeatedly inserted into and taken out of it.

You may be fortunate enough to have cast iron railings along the front of your window-sill, rather in the manner of a mini-balcony. These not only look good but are ideal for retaining, and even disguising, window boxes.

There is no reason why you should not put window boxes at all of your windows. The only proviso is that you should be able to reach the boxes because they will need to be watered nearly every day. In continental Europe it is not unusual to see houses of several floors festooned with boxes at every level, mostly bursting with bright scarlet geraniums. Apart from the fact that the owners probably like the colour of the geraniums, there is another, theoretical, reason for using brightly coloured flowers on tall buildings. Soft colours recede into the distance, and if you put a box full of soft blue and mauve flowers on the top floor it will look further away than it really is and appear quite indistinct. Bright colours, on the other hand, stand out and seem much closer. If you put soft blue petunias, for example, on the second floor they are going to appear too far away to be of any consequence. The red geraniums will show up like beacons. It is, of course, possible that you want to make your house seem taller than it is, and if that is the case, by all means use the softer colours at a distance – this is one of garden designer's oldest tricks.

As we noted above, once you get away from the ground floor, access is a problem. The tall houses of continental

Europe have boxes of geraniums on every floor simply because the windows open inwards. In Britain windows more often either open outwards or go up and down on sash cords. Sash windows present few problems to the window box gardener because access to the boxes is simple and convenient. An outward-opening window, however, will of course sweep everything from the sill every time it is opened. You can still use ground-floor sills because you can water from the ground outside, although you will not be able to open the window while the box is in position. A heavy window box might, in fact, be considered a deterrent to anyone try to break in through a window.

The problem arises with outward-opening windows on upper floors. If you own the whole house you can simply ignore these windows and concentrate your efforts on those that you can safely reach. However, if you live in a first- or second-floor flat, an outward-opening window could make it difficult for you to have the pleasure of having a window box. One way to overcome this is to fix the boxes directly to the wall, but below the level of the window. This does restrict the height of your plantings because obviously you cannot include tall plants that will come above the sill, but it does give perfect access for planting, watering and deadheading. The boxes must be fitted to the wall with strong brackets. They should not just rest on the brackets but be screwed firmly to them. Every time you replant a box, as well as giving it a thorough clean, you should check all the fixings to make certain that there is no rust or rot and that they are perfectly secure.

Boxes that are higher up can cause ugly stains on the wall where excess water has drained through. This can be a problem with a window-sill on the ground floor, but it tends not to be so noticeable, especially if there are plants growing in a border below. If you are worried about stains on the wall, it is best not to use boxes on the upper storeys at all. It is sometimes possible to fix a drip tray beneath the box so that water is shed outwards away from the wall, but the water is still likely to be blown back against the wall, although it will not be in such a concentrated area.

A balcony is an ideal place for locating window boxes. If the boxes are stood on the floor behind the railings or wall

This three-sill bay window has three similarly styled boxes linked by the swags of foliage beneath them.

they are perfectly secure, although they are unlikely to look their best. Railings are better than walls, because the plants can at least find their way between the bars and hang down. The best position is hanging from the top of the railings or wall, but this again presents the problem of security, because they must be firmly fixed in position and the means used to fix them must be regularly checked.

When the balcony is to be used as a mini-garden, the box should be on the inside of the balcony. If the box is to decorate the façade of the building, it should be fixed to the outside. If you are ambitious you can have one on each side of the railings or wall, doubling your display area. If the balcony has walls, the box could sit on top of the coping. This will allow it to be seen from both directions, but, again, it must be very firmly fixed because this is one of the most dangerous situations of all.

Balconies are perfect places for siting individual pots as opposed to long boxes. Rows of terracotta flowerpots, each

Flowers in strong colours stand out well against the white walls and completely hide the window boxes and sills.

containing a scarlet geranium, can be a splendid sight. There are many other plants that can also be grown in this way, but geraniums are always firm favourites. Even at the risk of labouring the point, it is important to stress that pots standing on a sill can be easily dislodged. Even a wind-free courtyard cannot be regarded as absolutely safe. It should be a fairly simple matter to put a metal or wooden bar across the window opening to prevent your containers from toppling off the sill. The bar need not be too thick, but it should be robust enough to support the weight of the containers.

Window boxes are so called because they are usually used to adorn windows. Although this is the most obvious place for them and they look most at home there, there are other places to consider. Balconies have already been mentioned, but there is no reason why they should not be used to brighten a section of blank wall. Perhaps you could fix two short boxes on either side of an otherwise dull doorway to cheer it up, or use a window box or two to brighten an ugly garage wall. The possibilities are endless.

One important factor when considering the siting of window boxes in whatever form they take, is that of aspect. Plants that are sitting in a box with relatively little earth around them to hold moisture and to keep the roots cool, and with the sun reflected back from the glass or wall behind them, combined with exposure to the wind, could hardly be in more difficult conditions. Most plants prefer a sunny position, but some find the conditions prevailing in and around a window box just a little too harsh. Regular watering helps, and doing so twice or three times a day is necessary when the weather is hot.

Many plants appreciate it if the box is protected during the very hottest part of the day. Fuchsias, pansies, begonias and busy lizzies, for example, all prefer at least a little bit of shade. They are happiest where they get just the morning and evening sun. They are even happy to grow on the north side of a building as long as they are not in too much shade, but it is worth bearing in mind that plants located on the north side of a building will inevitably grow towards the light and will become more drawn than those in boxes on a sunny façade.

Wind is an important consideration and not simply because of the security of the container. Strong winds can blow plants about and quickly reduce them to tatters. Some sides of a building are more likely to be subject to the prevailing winds than others. If you are planting a box that is going to be in a windy spot, avoid tall plants with soft growth that is likely to snap. Tough wiry plants, such as verbenas, are better suited to such positions. You should also avoid long, trailing plants. Ivies will get battered and may look tatty but will survive; softer growing plants, such as nasturtiums, can be devastated by high winds.

Draughts, which often occur between two buildings, should also be taken into consideration. Even on apparently still days, some areas seem especially prone to breezes and unexpected gusts of air. While most plants will tolerate some wind, few like being in a constant draught. If you are siting a window box in such a position take care to choose robust plants that will withstand such conditions.

One aspect of the positioning of window boxes that is often overlooked is scent. On the whole, window boxes are designed for their colour rather than for their smell, but because they are next to windows they are ideal places to plant fragrant flowers. Evening is the best time for most garden scents, so try siting a window box containing fragrant plants near a window of a room that is used at that time of day. Tobacco plants are an obvious example of the type of plants to use, and the box need not be full of scented plants – one or two among the more usual non-fragrant varieties is usually sufficient to perfume a room.

As you walk about a town or village, keep an eye on the buildings and you will be surprised at the ideas you will get about siting and planting of your boxes. The foregoing may make window boxes seem a terribly complicated business, but they are not. As long as you use your common-sense, there is no reason you cannot have the most delightful displays.

A simple, overflowing window box that is well suited to the style of window and surrounding planting.

Planting and maintenance

IN MANY RESPECTS window boxes come as near to being maintenance free as any kind of gardening is ever likely to, but, even so, there are still certain tasks, notably watering, that must be carried out regularly to ensure that you have a good display. How far you get involved with the propagation and growing of the plants depends on your facilities and the time you have available. These aspects of gardening require surprisingly little space, and the time you will need to spend is out of all proportion to the satisfaction of knowing that the magnificent display outside your window was the result of nothing more than a few packets of insignificant looking seed. With window boxes you can do as much or as little as you like or are able.

OBTAINING PLANTS

There are two approaches to obtaining the plants for your window boxes. The first is to go to your nearest garden centre or nursery and buy whatever plants you find there, and then set about planting them in the most attractive way you can. The other approach is to plan what you want to do and then go out and get the plants to fulfil your ideas. Both methods have their advantages, but the latter is preferable because you will end up with boxes that are much better balanced.

Ideas for designs will come from your own imagination, from illustrations in books and from boxes that other people have created. When you are thinking about your own plans, however, do not simply look at other people's window boxes – you are just as likely to get an idea from other types of container planting and even from borders and whole gardens. When you are out and about, keep your eyes open and carry a notebook to jot down ideas that appeal to you.

When you have decided what you are going to do, you can either grow the plants yourself and or buy them at a garden centre or nursery. The great thing about growing them yourself, apart from the satisfaction that the process gives, is that your choice of plants is so much greater. A garden centre may be able to offer you a pack of mixed petunias, but a seed merchant's catalogue will list 20 or more different mixtures and single-coloured flowers.

Seed is not the only method of growing plants, of course. Cuttings taken the previous autumn from plants such as geraniums and busy lizzies will provide a large number of plants at very little cost. Propagating on this scale really needs a greenhouse or cold frame, however, but it is surprising what can be done on the window-sill in the kitchen or spare bedroom.

If you do not have the space or the time to grow your own plants, most of the basic plants are readily available from garden centres and nurseries, even if the choice is not as large. When you are choosing plants, always select those that look healthy and are free from disease. Try to avoid any plants that look drawn or sickly. Whenever possible, choose a plant that has some flower on it so that you can check that the colour is right, but avoid those that are fully in flower because they might not develop properly once you have planted them out. Do not buy them too early if you have nowhere to store them out of late frosts.

If you have the space to grow plants of your own, you might also want to take the opportunity to prepare plants that you will use over and over again. For example, you could train some small box trees so that, if you require them, you have them ready. It is also a good idea to have some pots of trailing ivy growing on, because a display may be spoilt while you wait for undersized ivies to produce a good show of trailing stems.

PLANTING

Although there are a few rules for successful planting successful window boxes, they are not particularly complicated and you will still probably achieve satisfactory results if you ignore them, with one exception. If you want to grow lime-hating plants – heathers and skimmias, for example – it is crucial that you use a lime-free (ericaceous) compost.

Before putting the compost in the window box, however, you should look at the container itself. One of the most important aspects from the planting point of view is that there are drainage holes. In spite of constantly needing water, very few plants can stand being waterlogged. The amount of water that compost holds is the ideal amount from the point of view of the plant, and any extra should be allowed to drain away and not stand around the roots of the plant. If the roots are left in waterlogged compost, they cannot get any air, which is vital if the plant is to survive.

If a window box has no drainage holes, you will have to drill some in the lowest points of the base. This is not difficult if the container is made of wood or plastic, but it is more of a problem with ceramic containers. Theoretically, it is possible to have an inner box with drainage holes and an outer one without, so that excess water drains from the actual planted area into a sump. The difficulty here is that in periods of prolonged rain the sump may fill up beyond the base of the planted container, rotting the plants inside. When the window boxes are placed on sills or shelves, they should stand on blocks or short legs of some sort, so that the water can drain freely from the box.

As has been noted, window boxes, especially terracotta ones, can be very heavy when they are filled with compost. Unless you are very strong or have help, therefore, it is a good idea to place the box where you want it to flower and fill it in situ, rather than to fill it elsewhere and move it into position. Although filling the container with compost and plants before it is positioned on a sill is, in many respects, the better option because it gives the plants chance to settle and come into flower, do consider the difficulties of moving a heavy box and the damage you may do to yourself as you struggle and strain to lift it.

Apart from the holes that will allow excess water to drain away, good drainage within the box is vital, and when you are filling a box this must always be the first consideration. The drainage holes are there to let water out, but if you are not careful they may allow the contents to be washed out or they may even become clogged with compost and thus prevent water from draining away – sometimes both happen. To avoid this, cover the holes with pieces of old pottery (traditionally pieces of broken flowerpots usually known as crocks) or pieces of tile or irregularly shaped stones. You must cover the holes, but not so closely that the water cannot escape.

Another way that the free passage of water can be aided is to include a layer of drainage material. The most convenient material, because it can be bought at garden centres and do-it-yourself stores, is gravel or some other form of small stones such as chippings. The layer should be about 2.5cm (1in) deep.

The next layer is the compost in which the plants are grown. Gardeners are confronted with a bewildering choice of growing media when they get to the garden centre, and it is

This boldly coloured box of begonias is simple but very effective.

123

sometimes difficult to avoid the belief that the many variations on offer are more to do with getting gardeners to part with their money than with helping them to grow better plants.

There are two basic types of compost – soil-based, which is often referred to as John Innes, and soil-less. Soil-less composts used to be peat based but now, because of ecological concerns about the removal of vast quantities of peat from the countryside, a range of peat substitutes is used, including coir or coconut fibre. As their name suggests, the main ingredient of the soil-based composts is soil, which is supplemented with peat or peat substitute to hold moisture and with sharp sand or grit to keep the soil drained and sweet. Added to this are regulated amounts of fertilizer. The soil-less composts consist almost entirely of peat or a peat substitute. Some sand is added to help with drainage, and because peat (unlike soil) has no nutritional value, the compost incorporates quantities of chemical fertilizers to feed the plants. There are also other lightweight composts that you might consider. These contain substances, such as vermiculite, which hold quantities of water and yet at the same time aid drainage.

The relative merits of the different composts are much debated and both have their fervent advocates. Soil-based compost is heavy, it retains water well while being well drained and is easy to re-wet if it becomes dry. Soil-less composts are light in weight (a plastic window box with a soil-less compost is easy to lift but can easily be blown away when dry), are easy to over-water and are very difficult to re-wet once they have dried out. This last problem can be overcome if a pot dries out because it can be stood in a bucket of water to soak, but this is not practical solution with a window box. On balance, soil-based composts are preferable for window boxes, but the final choice must rest with the grower. See what your plants prefer and stick to it.

A special type of compost, specially formulated for use in containers of various kinds, including hanging baskets, contains water-retaining granules, which reduce the amount of watering that is required.

One last aspect of composts to emphasize is that if you are growing a lime-hating plant in a container you must have a lime-free (ericaceous) compost. Rhododendrons, heathers, skimmias and begonias all need acid conditions, and it is no good trying to grow them in a conventional compost that contains lime.

With the drainage material in place in the bottom of the window box, fill the remainder of the box to the brim. Do not press it down too much at this stage. Work out and mark the positions for the plants before planting. If you just begin to insert the plants at one end, you will probably plant them too far apart or too close together and have to start again. Dig holes and set in the plants, firming gently as you go. If any of the plants have large rootballs, there may be too much compost in the window box and you may have to remove some of it. The plants should be planted to the same depth as they were in their original containers.

There are two possible methods of including bulbs in your arrangements. The first is partly to fill the window box and then place the bulbs in position before continuing to add the compost. If you are adding other plants, mark the position of the bulbs so that you do not over-plant them. An alternative is simply to dig a hole and insert the bulb. Bulbs that are already growing in pots should be treated in this way. In general, the larger the bulb, the deeper it should be planted. A useful guideline is to cover a bulb with at least twice its own depth of compost. Cyclamen are an exception to this rule. They should be planted so that the top of the corm is level with the surface of the compost. To get a really luxuriant display of bulbs, plant them on two levels, so that the lower layer grows through the first.

Once all plants are in, gently firm down the compost but do not compress it too much. Then level the surface, either adding or subtracting compost so that the final level is about 2.5cm (1in) below the rim. While you are handling the plants, you are bound to upset the natural fall of the stems, so gently ease the stems and shoots into natural positions, allowing trailing stems to fall over the front of the box or weave in and out of the other plants.

Finally water the box, being careful not to crush the plants.

The box is now ready. There is nothing more to be done if you have filled it in situ. If you have the facilities, boxes or the inner cases of boxes can be prepared in a greenhouse or conservatory, and this is a particularly useful way of getting an early display. Many bedding plants cannot be put out until after the threat of the last frosts has passed, and by growing them under glass you can protect your young plants so that by the time your neighbours are planting their containers yours are already in full growth and showing masses of flowers. Remember though, that a fully planted container is difficult to move.

MAINTENANCE

Although window boxes are relatively trouble free, they do need some attention. The most arduous task is watering, and in spite of a few short cuts, there is really no way round it – it has to be done.

Your aim is to keep the compost moist without soaking it. This means a regular watering either from a can or a hose if there is no rain. Do not assume, just because it has rained, that the window box has received enough moisture. Because they are close to the house and often inset into the window recess, window boxes can often be completely dry after rainfall.

Whether you prefer a watering can or a hose, do not use too coarse or too violent a spray or jet. This will batter and bruise the plants, which not only makes them look unsightly but also allows diseases and infections to take hold. Watering boxes that are positioned on ground-floor window-sills is not usually a problem, but boxes on other floors can be more difficult, and the problem is compounded if you have outward-opening windows and the box is sitting on the sill. Rather than getting a ladder each time, a hose pipe can be fitted with a pole, or you could use one of the special hooked watering pumps that are designed for hanging baskets as long as the boxes are not too far from the ground.

You must water when you need to, irrespective of the time of day, but it is generally recommended that you water in the evening when the sun has lost its power so that droplets of water on the foliage do not act as small lenses and scorch the leaves, causing disfiguring brown patches. In spring and

A very colourful box with a bit of everything mixed in. Such unrestrained enthusiasm is a joy as long as the plants are well maintained.

summer, when plants are in full growth, they are likely to use vast quantities of water, and you will have to be prepared to water at least once a day, and when it is really hot even two or three times a day. Keep an eye on the compost and water as soon as it starts to dry out. Flagging leaves are a good sign that more moisture is required.

Growth slows down in autumn and not quite as much moisture is required, although you should be ready to provide water every day. In winter the soil does not dry out as fast as it does in summer, and the plants do not need as much moisture, so water carefully and only when the compost shows signs of drying out. But beware: the combination of a bright sun and strong wind on even a midwinter's day can dry out a box remarkably quickly.

It is now possible to buy water-retaining granules that can be added to the compost. These hold several hundred times their own weight in water and release it as the compost dries out – the manufacturers claim that they reduce the need water by up to three-quarters. They do, in fact, reduce the number of times you need to water the containers, but, of course, they still need the same total amount of water, so you need to provide extra every time you water, and you will still have to keep an eye on the compost, because on hot days you will need to water every day, even if you can ease up to every other day during dull weather. As we have seen, it is possible to buy special compost with the granules already incorporated in it. There are also some plastic, self-watering window boxes on the market, which may be worth looking into if you feel they will help.

The other essential task is to feed the plants. Plants cannot live on water alone, and although the compost will contain a certain amount of nutrients, often in the form of slow-release fertilizer, the constant watering will mean that the fertilizer is soon be washed or leeched from the soil. It is essential to replace it.

The easiest way to do this is to use a liquid feed. which is simply added to the water in the watering can and applied with it. In winter little growth takes place and it is not as necessary to feed as during the summer. When the plants come into growth, however, and when more water is being poured through the compost, you will need to feed regularly. The dosage will vary according to the plants – it may be twice a week or it may be every 10 days. Advice is given with each box.

As you water a box, take the opportunity to look closely at the contents. Remove any dead or dying flowers and cut off any straggly or unsightly stems. Pansies, for example, will re-shoot if an untidy plant is cut back almost to the base. It may be necessary to cut back some plants in order to keep the symmetry of a display. Topiaried shrubs, such as box, will need the occasional trim.

Sometimes a plant will die simply because it is naturally short lived or because it has been attacked by some pest or disease. At other times plants come to the end of their flowering season or are caught by a frost. All of these should be replaced by fresh plants as long as the rest of the display is still looking in good heart. If you expect some plants to have short lives and will need to be replaced, it is usually a good idea to plant them in pots rather than directly into the compost. These pots are then plunged into the compost. (They will need individual watering.) When the time comes to replace them, simply lift out the pot and replace it with another. This operation will be easier if you always use the same size of pot.

Pests and diseases are one of the curses that most gardeners would rather be without. On the whole, window box gardeners have little to worry about. The displays are relatively short lived in any case, and the compost is changed regularly so there is little chance of disease building up. If something nasty does happen it is not too expensive to discard the lot.

The best way of preventing trouble is to take precautions. Always use fresh compost, do not buy or use diseased plants and always remove any dead or dying material on which pests and diseases might breed. Watering and feeding your plants to keep them healthy helps a great deal. Sickly, malnourished plants are much more likely to succumb to attack. The most likely problem is going to be aphids or greenfly, but if you check every time you water, you should be able to forestall any major problem. If there are only one or two aphids, pick them off. If there are more you may have to resort to a spray, but do follow the instructions on the packet and spray only the part of the plant that is infested.

Once the flowers begin to flag and the plants get past their best, it is time to break up the display. Throw away all the annuals, but if you wish, take cuttings from such plants as the geraniums and fuchsias to create new plants to be used next year, and keep all the more permanent features, such as the box trees, miniature conifers and the like. All the old compost should be thrown away or added to the garden; use fresh when you replant. Thoroughly clean the box and examine it carefully for any rotting wood or rust on any of the fixings.

You are now ready to start again.

Index

Page numbers in *italics* refer to illustrations

PHOTOGRAPH ACKNOWLEDGMENTS

John Fielding 15, 25, 27, 55, 57, 59, 93, 110, 119, 123; **John Glover** 6, 7, 17, 19, 29, 49, 51, 67, 85, 97, 99, 101, 109, 111, 112, 121; **Jerry Harpur** 23; 13, 21, 41, 83, 120 (Susie Ind, Pimlico Flowers); **Marcus Harpur** 37, 39 (RHS Chelsea Show, 1995), 43 (Mary Harpur), 45 (RHS Chelsea Show, 1995); **Andrew Lawson** 9, 11, 47, 61, 63, 65, 87, 89, 91, 95, 105, 107, 108, 114, 117; **Clive Nichols** 79, 103 (The Lygon Arms, Gloucestershire); **Photos Horticultural** 31, 71, 73, 75, 77, 81, 125; **D Toyne** 53; **Ward Lock** 33; **Steve Wooster** 3, 35, 69.